Recess with Jesus

Games We Play with God

Aidan Rogers

ISBN: 146641488X

ISBN-13: 978-1466414884

To the Author who allowed me to borrow
these words. For Your mercy, Your grace,
  and Your gift, I eternally praise You.

Games to Play

| Prologue

It started with a game of "To Tell the Truth" in the garden, when God first questioned man about sin. A new relational dynamic emerged as man and Maker compared apples to apples.

We've been playing games with God ever since.

Even the giants of our faith rolled the dice. In their intimate encounters with the Living God, characters from the Old and New Testaments alike faced their Father head-on in battles of wits, fits, and hits.

Jacob wrestled with a stranger in the dark of night, battling for what he must have believed was his own life. Knowing nothing of his opponent, he took him down until the man cried "Uncle" and dawn arose with a new heavyweight champion – Israel.

Few, if any, of us would be so brazen. Perhaps even Jacob would have backed down had he known the man's true identity. But most of our games with God don't play out in a physical confrontation in the backwoods.

They come in the light and the fire of life in our desperate attempts to find an upper hand somewhere.

Take Lot's wife. The Lord's messenger came to rescue her family, to send them out ahead of destruction. She seized the moment, running into the hills with her husband and children. But she bet her life on the chance God was bluffing.

He wasn't.

Israel dared God to deliver them. He double-dared them to just trust. When they couldn't rise to the occasion, they were forced to take a physical challenge – forty years wandering in the wilderness.

God sent Jonah to raise the values in Nineveh. Jonah thought the price was right for the town's destruction and refused to go. God, in turn, sent Jonah on a whale of a ride.

It was the only time in history that the ride, not the rider, threw up.

And the first amusement where no one was amused.

The Pharisees took on Christ Himself in a game of twenty questions. More like twenty thousand questions.

Even at the foot of the cross, as the Lord hung by His hands and feet, the Roman guards cast lots for His clothing. I shudder to think of the poor guy who rolled a Yahtzee and took home a new pair of used underwear.

This was outright mockery, sitting at His feet and divvying up His possessions by mere chance. A gamble. A game.

But are we really any better?

There is a haughtiness in our game play. It is an insolent pride that boldly questions the very nature of God and errantly assumes we possess the strength, power, wisdom, or skill to share the court with the Almighty.

We, like Lot's wife, wonder if God is bluffing. Is He Who He says He is? Even His greatest gifts, we take with a grain of salt. We waver back and forth between simply accepting His graciousness and entertaining the notion, in the backs of our minds, that just possibly, this could be a test. He dares step down from Heaven to answer our hearts, to respond to our earnest prayers, and we cannot accept even that. Because He might not be Who He says He is. Or Who We pray He is. Or Who we believe He is. Or God at all; He could be Satan in disguise.

So we sit down at the table and play a few hands, trying to get Him to slip up and show His cards. Just so we know what He's playing with here.

The problem is that as much as we want to trust Him, to know that He is Who He is, the world says that's not how we play.

The world says we are powerless if our life is not in our hands.

The world says we need to know what comes next. We need to plan for what's coming down the road.

The world says we are foolish as we talk, pray into the silence wondering if anyone hears us.

The world laughs at our inadequacy in not knowing what to ask for, pray for, which door to knock on, which path to seek. The world says we can't live without our fear, pain, doubt, anger, selfishness, spite, pride, or any of the other million godless compasses that lead our self-guided journey.

These are the tokens we play with – not a top hat or a Scottie dog, an iron or a shoe, but the godless vegetables of the anti-Spirit. These are the pieces we move around the board. Rather, that move us.

Then we wonder why there's little joy in that $200 for passing Go.

That $200 used to make us happy. It used to provide security, an upper hand, a place and a prominence we thought unmatchable. It was our ticket to keep playing. But as the game wears on, the odds fall out of our favor. Assets slip through our fingertips as other players fill the board. All the good treasures are taken and somewhere down the line, we'll owe a luxury tax for living the high life too long.

Our desolation comes quickly; our defeat swift and certain. With a deep sigh, we pass the dice to God again for no other reason than respect for the game. The rules say we take turns; our turn is up, and it is God's now.

He rolls... just the right number to land on our one lonely square, to bide us time and continue the game.

Snake eyes.

He rolls again. Once more, He dances around the final blow, hopping and skipping His way through the board like an expert.

Our turn. Snake eyes. We're dangling by a thread here, running low on everything that used to sustain us, watching our tokens of godlessness dance around the board.

We pray God takes the final roll and ends it now. We pray not for the miracle that might save us; we've too long ago given up on miracles. No, we just want the game to end.

It's not fair! we cry. Everything was going so well. Why am I losing?

Now it's really not fair as God rolls just the right number to spare us, to give us another turn.

He's playing games with us!

The difference is that God is a benevolent player, the quintessential chess master in the park who embraces the teachable moments while He's beating the pants off us.

Those teachable moments come more often, and more unexpectedly, than we anticipate. One thing is certain: where we play for blood, God plays for mercy.

The Israelites found their footing after forty years in the desert. Then, God taught them to build a temple. The world kept knocking over their blocks, demolishing their handiwork, scattering the stone and the people themselves. Each time, God brought them back and gathered new blocks, returning the tools they needed to rebuild and guarding their efforts, but leaving the labor to His people.

They learned the value of the cornerstone.

Job became God's pawn in a cosmic game of chicken. I'm sure that's how he must have felt about it, even though he didn't know the power play that Satan was trying to make through Job's trials. Through a life of faith and the imparting of God's wisdom, Job was perfectly primed for this challenge. He may not have known exactly what was going on, but he knew the commission God had given him: never back down.

He learned the reward of blind faith.

With the timer set on Belshazzar's reign, a cosmic hand scribbled on the wall. The party guests looked around, stunned, wondering who brought Pictionary. They hadn't even finished the meal! Completed, the picture revealed just four words: "Mene. Mene. Tekel. Parsin."

I imagine God on His throne, throwing His hands in the air, exclaiming, "Geez! Do I have to draw you a picture?"

Sometimes, He does.

The Lord ordained the first ever game of kick Baal.

And God, the original team captain, always filled His roster with those we'd expect to be last-picked, if ever picked at all.

He started His line with an old woman, far too old to have children, or so we thought. He commanded perhaps the only man crazy enough to listen to build an ark and gather animals.

Yes, Noah. Even the snakes and every type of bug. *Two* of every bug.

A little shepherd boy not big enough for war, the last son of Jesse who almost went overlooked even by the prophet sent to anoint him, the little scrawny boy stuck out in the fields with the sheep, in the dirt and the heat and the loneliness, slew a giant became Israel's greatest king, a man after God's own heart, and one of the foremost fathers of our faith.

A stutterer to speak for the Lord. A prostitute to shield His armies. A meek prophet to control the rain. A virgin to carry His only Son. And a Nazarite – a *Nazarite* for Heaven's sake – to redeem the world. A persecutor and a Roman to spread His message. An exile to pen His prophecy.

These are not the people anyone would expect to make the team, especially not first-string, first-picked. That alone tells us how God plays the game. He does not judge a worthy contender by any of our standards – by strength or size or experience or intelligence.

He judges by wisdom, courage, obedience, and discipline. These make worthy contenders; these make men and women welcome to occupy His table. These, the chess master Himself takes under His wing to transform, teach, and mold.

They listen in the teachable moments. They soak in the understanding of the Master. They grow and blossom and learn, and they always return to the table. Not as we are – not bloodthirsty, out for domination, in it only to win it.

They return for the lessons. For the sake of the game.

This is what gives them the right to guide generation upon generation of God's people through their stories preserved and passed down. This is what gives them the opportunity to ask questions, to challenge God, to prod and poke and pray to understand His ways. This is what gives them the gall to approach Him boldly, asking, seeking, and knocking with no pretense.

This is what makes them champions.

How do we get from the childish, selfish, godless games of Lot's wife and the Pharisees to the Master's table? What are the games we too often play, and how do we find it in ourselves to pass the dice and accept these teachable moments, even when it means losing?

We have to stop thinking about losing and instead be willing to forfeit. To turn the dice over to the One we are all hoping – deep within us – will win anyway. Despite our posturing, our bragging, our obstinacy and defiance and ego, our childish temper tantrums, and yes, even our cheating, we *want* Him to win.

That's what makes the game worth playing. That's what makes us venture onto the playground day after day after day. Not that we might one day win, but that we will one day learn and find the answer we were looking for all along:

God is. He absolutely, truly, one-hundred-percent, eternally, and completely is everything we've hoped and prayed and begged Him to be. We can play by His rules and still win. A little more faith, a little less self, a little understanding, sacrifice and forfeit, and we find our victory.

Sacrifice is tough. Faith is tough. Selflessness is hard and counter to our culture. But without that sacrifice, we know the games we'll play.

We'll keep stacking the deck and dealing the cards.

We'll keep rolling the dice.

We'll keep picking the tokens of deity, fear, pain, anger, selfishness, and the other godless idols that run our lives.

We'll play to win without realizing we lose.

1 | Capture the Flag

"Therefore, go and make disciples of all the nations, baptizing them in the name of the Father and the Son and the Holy Spirit." - Matthew 28:19

Storm the world. Steal their banner and replace it with God's, then hold high your trophy as a symbol of your triumph. These are the dreams evangelists are made of.

It is our Great Commission, our most clearly stated divine order to spread out and infect the world. It is our permission to seek out darkness and conquer it with Light, and like most things, we believe this can only be done with the loudest voice or the greatest force. We charge forward blindly, our eyes focused on the prize – the banner flying high above the world declaring its allegiance to self.

This is what the world boasts in, and this is the basis for its delusions of invincibility - the more that man trusts in himself, the less likely he is to be shaken. The more he controls his own destiny, the more adaptable he becomes to handle life's inconsistencies.

God admonishes us to tear down that flag, to offer an alternative that will raise His colors high and free the world from its own inconsistencies.

Some of us would rather not accept this call; we don't understand why it isn't enough to stay in our own camp – God's camp, that happy little place we call church and good living – and simply defend His name. Certainly, there is a place in God's army even for this group, but it is still not a passive role.

Let us never forget that while we pursue the world, the world is pursuing us, trying to tear down our banner and take our faith hostage.

When something of the world comes against God, it is not enough to push it away and seek refuge in His castle. Even for those of us who play defense, we must be ready to engage in battle. We must take captive the attacker and expose them to life under God's law so that they can see the contrast between their flag and His. We must demonstrate the difference between their army and His, show them the beauty of the discipline He instills in His forces, and invite them to make their own decision. Turned loose, they are welcome to stay not as prisoners but as recruits. Or they can return to the disarrayed world and their old colors.

For those of us who take this Great Commission to heart and set out to boldly evangelize the world, we run the risk of returning as wounded warriors. That is because we set out without a clear plan of attack, without strong weaponry, and without a clear understanding of what it means to be on God's strike team.

Our plan of attack is simple. We commit to taking the world by force. We plan to storm through the darkest places like Christ in the Temple, turning everything upside down and creating such a scene that people have to notice. We resist or outright condemn the lifestyles of the godless, casting the people carelessly aside as mere collateral in our quest to stamp out the offending behaviors of greed, selfishness, homosexuality, or whatever mission of "cause" we think we are on.

We attack without a full arsenal, believing that the power of God in His own message is enough. What we know of Him and what is obvious to us about His nature should be enough. We charge by ourselves and expect one lone lunatic with a six-shot pistol is enough to change the world.

And when we charge, we run head-first toward the banner, our determination to fell it enough to power us through any obstacle.

If we are lucky enough to even reach the flag with these tactics, we are surrounded on our way out of enemy territory, while we hold the flag high above our heads and declare victory. The enemy pounces before we even take two steps, and we become the world's prisoner, a public display of that wacko rogue Christian who just doesn't get it.

This war is not a firefight where our bullets of truth win out. This is not a war where we'll win stepping out with guns blazing. No heart has ever been won by force.

This is guerrilla warfare.

To win this war, we have to be cunning. We have to move about in plain sight without being seen, without drawing attention to ourselves. We have to learn to blend into our surroundings without becoming a part of them. We have to embrace the people living under foreign rule and win them over while we pursue their dictator.

That is God's battle plan. It is not that we should go in and open fire aimlessly, shooting down whatever stands in our way. It is that we should enter with awareness and sensitivity to our surroundings, then work from the inside to subvert the world.

He tells us to return biting words with those of forgiveness and mercy.

He tells us to give more than the world thinks it is taking from us.

He tells us to let go of everything and share our bounty, share our manna and living water from the foxhole.

He tells us that when the world heaps a burden on our shoulders, to carry it further than they expect. We know we are better equipped because we know His strength carries us, and He shares our yoke.

This is not the way to defeat anyone, but it is a powerful tool in defeating everything. This is the strategy that allows us to develop allies, people who will come to trust us and our character in such a way that they will lead us to their flag, begging us to tear it down. They will hand over the very thing that has controlled and defined their lives because they desire to join a new army. They are tired of living as a slave, as the unwilling draftee who has no choice but to serve.

They will envy our relationship with our Commander in Chief, and they will long for His constant provision that accompanies us. In their zeal, these converts often make the same mistakes we made once upon a time. They run full speed in the open field and try to tear down the flag in full sight of everyone, and they are captured immediately and pulled back into the prison of the malevolent leader.

Our mission then becomes two-fold: pursue the banner and free the prisoner.

He arms us with the weapons to reveal His nature, a quiver full of the sharpest arrows of His word, His promises, His majesty, and His story. We can talk of His word, of prophecies fulfilled and covenants kept and His intervention in this world. We can speak of the way He created the world and then redeemed it to Himself because of His undying love for us.

We can propagate His promises, inviting others to experience His grace and mercy. We can elaborate on His forgiveness and His generosity, which extends even to our sometimes painful free will.

We can point out the work of His hands, the beauty of the trees swaying in the wind and the way the eagle glides through the clouds. We can share in the sunshine or the relief of the rain.

And we can recount His work in the lives of His people, in this generation and every generation before. We can teach the rescued prisoners the stories of the fathers of our faith, the wise women who set the stage for Christ's coming, the spread of His message of redemption through the world and the power of the resurrection for all the doubting Thomases. We can share His story in our story, His work in us.

These weapons of truth pierce all pretense and begin to establish a reverence for the Leader of our army, the Secretary of Defense Who has been writing His strategies and outcomes for thousands of years.

There is a final piece to God's battle plan, to the tactics that enable us to succeed in our Great Commission. It is that of joining forces, of being a part of God's team and submitting ourselves to community in something much bigger than ourselves.

No soldier wants to fend for himself on the front lines. He wants to be part of a team, part of the highly trained strike force where these other soldiers literally become family. Brothers and sisters.

That is why we cannot ignore the community God places us in. The strength and health of the church is absolutely vital to His mission.

The church is our base camp. It is the place where we reload our weapons and pack extra ammunition for the fight. It is the place where we receive our marching orders and clarify our mission.

There, the scouts report back on the strongholds of the opposition, their weaknesses, and their needs. Using this intelligence, we strategize to maximize our return, to reach the most people and free them from the tyranny of the world. How can we, as a community, reach this population? we ask back at headquarters. We map out the best uses of our Alpha team, each specially gifted member contributing to the mission and the multi-faceted attack.

Together, we storm the world, darting and dodging its assaults, armed to the teeth with the only weapon able to pierce the hardest hearts, and as part of a well-disciplined strike force discipled for just this occasion.

We finally reach the flag and tear it down, but we do not hold it high over our heads. We handle it gently, knowing its power over those who too long lived beneath it. We empathize, knowing that we once lived under this banner ourselves. Before God redeemed us.

In place of the fabric stained by sin, the simple white flag of surrender blows in the breeze. Perhaps these ex-fighters are not yet recruits in the army of God, but at the least, they are free from the tyranny of a fickle and unloving master.

Worship and praise echo through the field as we report back to our Commander in Chief. It was a work well done, but the victory is short-lived. Though prisoners walk free and hearts have been won, there will be no treaty, no retreat, nor no ceasefire. The leader of the enemy combatants is defeated but not destroyed, and he is already building his new regime.

The war rages on as a new flag rises over the opposing world. Our mission again to tear it down and fly a new flag.

We start as a lone sharpshooter living a quiet life in plain sight, a wacko rogue Christian willing to love deeply, forgive freely, embrace fully, and serve selflessly.

"If it seems that we are crazy, it is to bring glory to God. ...He died for everyone so that those who receive his new life will no longer live to please themselves. Instead, they will live to please Christ...." - 2 Corinthians 5:13a,15

2 | Chicken

"For when your faith is tested, your endurance has a chance to grow. So let it grow, for when your endurance is fully developed, you will be strong in character and ready for anything." - James 1:3-4

Strong in character and ready for anything. Paul adds that from perseverance, a first cousin of endurance, comes not only character, but hope. These are noble aspirations, the fruits of faithfulness we all long for.

Perhaps a little too much.

Particularly in recent times, our sense that God is testing us borders more on cynicism than the kind of growth opportunity James and Paul present. When things don't go our way or our hearts fall victim to disappointment, we are quick now to rush and blame God.

If He were listening... or if He really loved us... or if He didn't thrive on His own power and omnipotence, then He wouldn't toy with us like this. He wouldn't make us suffer rejection or disappointment or diversion if He understood the depth of the yearning in our heart. We conclude that He will, eventually, relent if only we survive this test.

If we continue to stand and show our dedication and our faithfulness, our unshakeable confidence that He is doing what we figure He is doing (or want Him to be doing), then He will reward our steady eyes with the prize.

That's got to be what's going on here; the object of our affections fits too perfectly with our plans or our hopes or our passions. This is a test; we know God is in the business of testing people. Ever read Job?

Job was the epitome of faithfulness and righteousness, and still God used him as a pawn in the most dramatic game of chicken ever played. He passed the test and withstood the devil's taunting, then God rewarded him with blessings too numerous to count.

We want blessings too numerous to count! We want the rewards of the faithful! We'll stand toe-to-toe with the devil as long as it takes to prove our righteousness.

Or so we say. But in all our fervor, it is often us who initiate the challenge. And it's not against our enemy; it is against our God. We boldly approach the throne of God and dare Him to disappoint us.

Here's our plan, we say as if He doesn't already know. This – this opportunity, this place, this affection, this circumstance, this victory, this whatever – is obviously Your plan for me, God. I know this even though I haven't bothered to ask You. It feels too right to be anything different. So I know You have this for me. It may not come today. It may not come tomorrow. But I promise, Lord, to hold onto this with all my heart until it comes to pass, that I can be an example to the world of faithfulness and Your goodness will show through me.

Right. Did you catch that little phrase in there that we often omit but might stop us dead in our tracks if we ever admitted it? "I haven't bothered to ask You," followed immediately by "it feels too right." We whittle God down to a feeling in our heart, an emotion, and clutch onto that with every tendon in our bony little fingers.

Worse, sometimes we pray anyway and seek God's will only to find "signs" that He's telling us what we already wanted to hear. An innocuous phone call, falling star, rain cloud, or song on the radio becomes the messenger of the Lord, sent to tell us that He's heard our prayer and is answering just exactly as we planned for ourselves.

It's not that He doesn't use these things to answer us; He certainly does. It's also not that He doesn't sometimes give us precisely the desires of our hearts; He does that, as well. It's that it is all too easy to fall into the trap of seeing what we want to see, of seemingly twisting God's arm into responding in a time or place He's not ready to speak yet.

We stand, defiantly, on our own promises, refusing to move until God fulfills them. Come Hell or high water, nothing will shake our faith or cause our hearts to question.

It's usually Hell.

It is little wonder, then, that more and more people – even those who fill the pews each Sunday – are growing disillusioned with God. He is not good, they say. He can't even deliver what He promises. He is spiteful or mean, a codgery old man sitting up in the heavens somewhere moving us around the Earth like pawns on a chess board for His amusement.

Cynicism. We have created God in our image and challenged Him directly, dared Him to deny us, and now we're disappointed that He is Who He says He is.

What it is that comes over us in that stance? Our feet are never more solid; our hearts never more resolved. Neither the harshest winds nor the loudest noise make us flinch. We could stand there forever holding onto hope as we wait for God to do what He never promised. This is the perfect faith that produces our endurance, that forms our character, and that builds our hope.

It just has nothing at all to do with God. He is the wind, the noise, the heat. He is the small speck of light behind our eyelids when we blink that causes us to shake our head when we open our eyes. Then, we gather our focus once more and stare right through Him, our posture unchanging and always challenging His goodness.

But He is good. A truly gracious God. We just blind ourselves to His "distraction," which is often His gift, by refusing to pray honestly, to listen earnestly, to budge or to back down.

In this posture, we are only testing our own faith and building an endurance that leads us away from strong character and away from hope. As time passes, the elements weather our bodies, but still we stand as our candle all but dies. We thought there was a God. Not just a God, but a good God who loved us and cared for us and worked in all things for our good.

He's only a figment of our imagination, we begin to think, and wonder if there might be truth to the cultural myth that each man is his own god. That if we truly wanted whatever we've been counting on faith for, we should have stalked it like a hungry lion instead of waiting patiently on the Lord. The Lord. Who is that, anyway?

Certainly not the good and gracious God we heard about in the pews.

Unless we adjust our posture and seek God being God, letting go of our insistence that He work as we would choose, this cynicism takes deep root in our hearts. It eats away at everything that once spurred us toward faithfulness, even our misguided or unhearing faithfulness.

Worse, by staying in our obstinate stance, we miss out on the absolutely wonderful things God is actually doing in our lives. We want this opportunity, and in our waiting, we miss out on a dozen others where God already opened the door and let fresh winds blow.

That breeze in our faces is just a temptation, we say and continue to stand defiant.

It is only the devil who wants to deny our greatness, we tell ourselves, and reject the voice of the One whose greatness we truly desire.

We pray and never hear an answer because that clatter is just the voice of the enemy trying to get us to back down; it is obvious to us this is where God wants us.

It is a battle of wills, a glorified staring contest where we pit the resilience of our heart against the wisdom and eternal patience of the Almighty. He rises to our challenge and answers our insistent stare.

But He never blinks.

He never wavers or takes His eyes off of us. He never taunts nor teases us into submission.

He doesn't just stand there, either. He's not about to succumb to our level and think for one minute that there is any good way to win this death match. No, He keeps moving and working and winding His way through our world. He works diligently, not necessarily to fulfill our desires but to create and propose alternatives.

Were we listening, we might hear His voice saying, "Look over here! An open window!"

Or "Do you hear that? Opportunity knocks!"

Or "Gosh, you look thirsty just standing there like that. Would you like a drink? A little sip? Well, I'll just leave the water here until you're ready for it."

Instead, we hear only the voices in our head, the ones that say, "Hold on just a little longer. Surely, God is working on this for you. It would be easy to quit now, but that is part of the test. That's part of faithfulness. Just a little longer, and your endurance will pay off. Your hope will be fulfilled!"

God's tireless work is His goodness. It's more than His wanting to break our stare for just a second, to entice us with the perfectly good and wonderful things He is offering. It's more than His silent refusal to engage in this silly showdown.

His work provides us a way out, a way to exit our stance and take a new path and a new posture without admitting defeat. He knows the longer we stand there with no encouragement, we're going to grow weary. We're going to feel the ache and the exhaustion. And we're going to get hungry.

The bounty He's busy spreading before us, to the left and the right or even opposite where we thought we were heading, is our banquet. It is a blessing that softens the blow of defeat.

We're not going to win, not against a God whose will is always good and never-changing. He knows that; so do we. It's just a matter of time before we come to our senses and give up, and God wants to make sure that when we decide to back down from our challenge, from our defiance and our demands and our childish insistence that borders on a temper tantrum, that we find something of Him immediately.

He knows we're likely to blame our loss on Him and abandon any pursuit of faith or character or hope, so He wants us to know, immediately, that He's still there and still good and still working on our behalf. He wants us to turn around and see a plethora of paths and open doors available to us, still a choice of free will to choose, but all good.

Then, it is He who stands firm, steady as a rock, watching us mindfully while we decide.

It is His goodness that gives us a better answer when our hopes do not come to fruition, when our labor seems in vain, and we find a world waiting for our response.

I thought God was leading me to go this way, we say when people inquire about our change of heart. But then, this other opportunity popped up out of nowhere, and I knew that's where He wanted me to go.

We blink and are blinded by His bounty. Bowing out of our mock competition, we take a new posture and pursue a new path. He has redeemed our endurance and built character, indeed, for we walk away neither defeated nor disheartened but more confident than ever that God is God and God is good.

"Human plans, no matter how wise or well advised, cannot stand against the Lord." - Proverbs 21:30

3 | Dodgeball

"As David played his harp for the king, Saul hurled his spear at David in an attempt to kill him. But David dodged out of the way and escaped into the night, leaving the spear stuck in the wall." - 1 Samuel 19:9b-10

So there we are, standing in the place we have always wanted to be. We are not comfortable, but we are content. There is a dramatic sense of peace and fulfillment in our lives; we know this is where God desires us to be. Maybe not forever, but for now.

From here, we are in harmony. We create beautiful music and sing the melody of praise that rises to the skies. This song draws the world to what we have, spurs them to seek God and join the chorus.

And then it happens. Out of the corner of our eye, we see it – a spear, hurtling toward our heads.

There is no mistaking that these spears were thrown at us. The light in which we had long been basking now reflects off the spear's sharp tip; its pointed message sails toward our heart and fear takes hold.

It is dangerous, a real threat.

We duck, but that doesn't seem sufficient, so we jump out of the way, twisting our bodies to the side in the nick of time. The spear soars past and lands somewhere behind us, having hit nothing of particular importance. But the damage is done.

Our song is silenced.

It takes more to silence some of our songs than others, but the culprit is the same: these are well-timed attacks from the enemy or simply from the fallen nature of our world. These attacks take advantage of our confidence and of the evidences of God in our lives, then sabotage them by forcing us to move out of that spot. Away from the place with perfect acoustics, where our song carries on the wind and resonates.

The arrow's trick is in our own light as the spear uses our radiance to intensify our fears. We see the reflection of our peace and our faith on its tip, speeding straight toward us, and we sense the danger.

If we stand our ground, that sharp point will run straight through our hearts and destroy us, shattering our song and stripping our worship. The reflected light blinds us to the coming threat so that we know our bubble is about to burst.

Behind that light, there could be something absolutely devastating. It could be the very thing that would pierce and destroy us. It could be something so powerful that it at least puts us in intensive care. It is a chance we cannot, or choose not to, take.

We follow the trajectory with our eyes, planning our move. This is not something we can go under, hunkering down until the threat passes. Nor is it something we can jump over, harnessing the power within us to take the high road and avoid its threat. We have to step aside.

In stepping aside, we give up our place. We give up our confidence and our worship that was so vibrant in that place. We give up our song.

But God keeps singing. He uses our own melody to call us back to that place. It is the place He created for us, the one where we encountered Him fully with mercy and grace and worship. It is the place where His presence set us aglow, where His glory intersected with our surrender. It is the place where we could not be shaken, where we stood firm.

Until the arrows started flying and we forgot everything that place meant to us.

Still, we long to return to that place. He calls us to stand again. But it is a place under constant assault, the place where we are sure to take on enemy fire. How can we step back in there? How can we return to the place of our confident assurance when that place seems to have lost all peace?

The enemy and the world want to keep us out of there. From all directions, threats fly every time we get close, full speed and menacing in their reflection of the light.

God knows we will not go where there is fear, where fear overrides our assurance in Him. He knows that if we are ever to get back to that place of deepest faith, we must first confront our fear. We have to pick it up, hold it in our hands, turn it around and around and understand that it is no match for Him.

He calls us to the field of fallen ammunition, where everything the world has sent against us lies futile. These weapons accomplished their mission without ever touching us; they got us to give up everything, abandon our place of perfect harmony, and step aside without a single hit.

Now that we hold it in our hands, we see that its threat was highly exaggerated. It is not as sharp as it first appeared, and we realize how the light let this weapon play a trick on our mind. In fact, it is rather dull and certainly no match for the shield of faith. It holds no heat, which means it was not fired with great force but instead hurled pathetically in our direction by something much lesser. It is rusty, dusty, dull, and useless. The only thing it ever would have been good for was inducing fear.

And in that, it succeeded.

Knowing first-hand that this could never have hurt nor destroyed us, we approach again the place where we once lived in perfect unison with God, where our song carried on the winds. With a deep breath, we return and plant our feet more firmly on the ground. We still wince when the attacks come near, but we steel our hearts. It is nothing more than our eyes playing tricks with us.

Our song returns, louder and more honestly worshipful than before. A spear flies in. We bend our body to the left or right and feel the spear as it whips past our ear, but we will not move. We are unafraid of anything this world throws at us. The most that any attack can do is cause us to strike a minor chord; in this place, it cannot destroy us.

Weaving the world's disappointments and devastations into our melody honors this place, this life, and this faith.

But God does not call us to be unafraid so that we can stand there and take the hits, over and over letting them knock our wind away or put a chink in our armor. He calls us to return the favor.

Throughout history, the story of God's people is that of them returning fire. They take whatever the world throws at them and do not just let it fall idly to the ground; they embrace it, filling it with the power of God and sending it right back.

Joseph's brothers sold him into the hands of Egyptian traders. He embraced his new role until the sting of betrayal faded and when famine struck, he returned the favor to his brothers and father in forgiveness and provision.

Gideon protected his supply of grain by stuffing it down into the winepress, where the Midianites could not touch it. Empowered by God to pursue the opposing army, Gideon set out and found the Midianite army stuffed down into a valley, where they were sure to be touched.

Mordecai was the target of a palace plot to destroy the nation of Israel. The official hung a gallows to hang the Jew, but God revealed this man's scheming and lynched the conniving official in his own noose.

These men did not step aside or try to avoid the assaults of the world, where they were obviously the targets and taking on heavy fire. They did not tuck tail and run to some place safe where they knew nothing could touch them.

Because they understood that any "safe" place where they were invincible would put them outside God's will, untouchable by God, and they were not willing to go there.

They were willing to stand boldly and take head-on what the world was dishing out, knowing that God would bless them with the chance to return the favor.

Even the Man central to our story, Christ, did not step out of the way, even though He wanted to get out of dodge. Before the guard arrived in the garden to arrest Him, He went off privately and prayed that it would not have to be this way. He prayed that if there was some other way, that it would come to pass.

But despite His reservations and His human reluctance, He knew that when this attack came, His role was simply to accept it. Embrace what God was doing in that moment. And use that opportunity as ammunition to return the favor, dealing a knockout blow to death itself.

The strength, peace, and confident assurance of Christ in Gethsemane and on the hill of Golgotha allowed Him to stand firmly in the place where His life intersected with God, where they sang a beautiful song together that echoed through the world. It allowed Him to embrace the persecution, the crown of thorns, the insults hurled at Him. And it allowed Him to return the favor by defeating death and turning the attack of the world into the greatest thing that ever happened to it.

That is what God calls us to do in our own lives. He calls us to relish the place He has for us so deeply that we are not willing to give it up for anything. He calls us to understand that our eyes may deceive us, that we may not understand what comes flying our direction or we may underestimate our ability to handle it. He calls us to stand there anyway, echoing the chorus of His song and ready to embrace what comes our way.

He calls us to accept what the world throws at us and to hold tightly to His promises so that through our hands, in firmness and faith and the mercy that courses through us, we can return the favor and hurl something more powerful and more threatening right back – Him.

Our return fire will shake the world. It will move them to the side. They will hem and haw, dart and dodge, but they will never escape untouched. The pointed message will be for them, the light of the Lord reflecting unmistakably off its tip. Darkness will shatter. Hearts will be pierced.

The song of the world will stop suddenly, and the faulty acoustics will show in the lack of any echo.

In the stillness that follows, all will know the glory, the goodness, and the grace of our God. And the song of the faithful, who stand firm in His promises and dare to return fire, will fill the air.

"He has given me a new song to sing, a hymn of praise to our God. Many will see what he has done and be astounded. They will put their trust in the Lord. Oh, the joys of those who trust the Lord..." - Psalm 40:3-4a

4 | Duck Duck Goose

"He lived in isolation, excluded from the Temple of the Lord." - 2 Chronicles 26:21b

A local church uses the tagline, "A Place Where Friends Gather." Most of us can identify with that. Church is the place where you know everybody and everybody knows you, where you have been through life together for sometimes decades, where you feel welcome and comfortable, and where the weights of the world are shared in a way that lightens everyone's load.

Church is a brotherhood and a sisterhood. It is friendship, and it is family. These congregants, pastor and lay person, elder and deacon, friend and new member, comprise faith's social circle.

But we never make the circle big enough. Church is supposed to be community, a conglomerate of faith that has a place for everyone to worship, love, strengthen, serve, and be served. Still, there always seems to be someone left on the outside, looking for a place to join in but never quite getting there. They try to squeeze between this person and that, but there is no room there. No room on the other side, either.

There are many reasons we find ourselves on the outside at church. Sometimes, we are the new kid. We have recently joined a ministry or the church as a whole, and we do not know many of the members yet.

In our search for a place, we have found this group of magnetic friends who seem like the kind of people we want to be around, the group we want to belong to. We just have to find a way to break in.

Sometimes, we may be excluded because of our situation. Maybe we live in the poor end of town when at church, we are surrounded by suburbanites. Maybe our best tithe doesn't make a dent in the church's needs. Maybe our clothes aren't the latest fashions or we haven't had a new style since the 1980s. Some things seem to inherently set us apart from the group and whether it is the group that rejects us or our own sense of shame that binds us, we feel like outsiders.

There are times where circumstance leaves us out of the circle. We all fight battles, and those battles can take us away from the very support we need. It could be an ugly divorce or family situation. Or a prolonged illness in the family, perhaps our own. Or maybe we just find ourselves questioning and choose to withdraw for awhile and seek answers in solitude. When our time away is over, we come back to find a group that has closed the circle in our absence or filled the space we once occupied, and we wonder how we will ever fit back in.

It is not that we lament losing our old place, for we know how our circumstance has changed us; we would never fit there again. But it pains us how difficult it can be to find any place at all.

Regardless of how we found ourselves on the outs, we yearn to find our way in.

The simple solution is to pick a role model, someone who already has a place in the circle, and pursue him or her in the hopes that we can wiggle into their place or at least meet them there and squeeze in together. We never pick the newest member of the group or the Sunday morning faithful, the ducks. We pick someone strong in the faith, someone involved in the work of the church who can guide us to a position of ministry or service, or at least get us noticed again.

The goose.

There is some honor in chasing the goose; it makes us more likely to achieve goose status ourselves, to one day be the one chased by those seeking their place in our circle of faith.

But fresh out of the gates, we can hardly keep up. We run ourselves ragged in pursuit of the goose, though their gait is steady and ours more frantic. We have not fallen into the rhythm of honest service but are harried by trying to prove ourselves. Before we even close the gap, our goose has rediscovered his or her place in the circle.

Again and again, we single them out and relentlessly chase their place. They always beat us back there, always slip seamlessly into the group. For all our effort and persistence, we gain nothing. We gain no place, not even an honorable mention. People are not impressed by our sweat, and we wear ourselves out until we are completely burnt out on the idea of doing anything.

Disappointment sinks in; we feel worthless. There is no work in the church for us, no special niche in the community of faith that could use our touch. No one notices if we show up or stay home. No one reaches out to us. No one invites us in. No one even likes us.

At this point, we would be happy just to be a duck!

Then, bitterness grows. What's wrong with these people? we ask. Don't they understand the tremendous contribution I can make? Don't they know how my heart longs to serve, to be active in their work, to further the cause of Christ? Whatever I lack in skill, I make up for in passion... and then some.

Over time, we resent our position in life that left us outside of the circle – the newness of our faith, our personal situation, the circumstances of life. These are the things that prohibited us from being all we were called to be. These are the reasons we get winded and fall short. We wonder if it is worth chasing the goose any more, worth continuing the struggle for a place. And often, we withdraw from the church. Maybe we do not cut our attendance altogether, but maybe we become a Sunday morning seat filler rather than a member of the community.

God understands our disappointment here, and He is saddened by our conclusions. For He never sent us on a wild goose chase.

That is a goose we could never catch.

In all His wisdom, God created each individual to be unique, with a certain calling and an unquenchable passion to serve Him according to our heart. The reason we will never catch our goose and will never take that place in the circle is because that is not our place.

It is not our place to copy what someone else is already doing well, even if that is what makes them stand out to us. Our goose may be someone else's duck – and we may be both a duck and a goose. It is not our place to try and fill a space that is already filled; that leaves someone else on the outside wondering what happened. And we, who know intimately the pain of being an outsider, should never cast that fate on anyone.

It is our place, however, to pursue our passions. It is our place to pray faithfully and discern God's call that will lead us to our place. When our exhaustion, disappointment, and bitterness at never catching our goose fades, we find that the ache is still there – the deep longing to be a part of God's community, to be active and involved, to reach the world.

This incurable ache leads us back to God. It leads us to question His plan for us, to beg for our calling revealed. It leads us to forgive ourselves for our situation or our circumstance, to forgive others for not responding as we had hoped. It leads us to understand both the beauty and the brokenness in the same church that too long provoked us to bitterness.

It leads us to stand before the throne of God. Maybe we are standing alone, hearing the busyness of the church somewhere off in the distance. Maybe there is nothing but us and the Cross, created and Creator. Maybe it is lonely, but it will not be forever.

The more we stand out there by ourselves, staring away from the church and directly into the eyes of God, the more likely it is that someone will come and invite us to be a duck. Someone will ask us to play a bit part in something they are doing or invite us to a small group or Bible study. Someone will decide to make a place for us.

But we have already found our place. Our place is here, before God, fully engrossed in Him and fully surrendered.

And when we stand honestly, vulnerably, fully before the throne of God and invite His work, His Word, and His will into our lives, we are bound to become somebody's goose.

Someone will leave that closed circle of the church and come over to see what we are up to. There, they will encounter the same God we are encountering, and no words will be spoken. There will be no invitations to come back as a duck, and they will not miss the place they used to hold. Together, two will stand before God in discipline and devotion.

One goose turns to two, and then a whole flock of geese gather at the foot of the cross. The circle that once held tightly to itself has opened up and provided space for all who would come. Come they will, for this gaggle of geese is a mighty force, calling on the ducks of the world who aspire to something more, who long to find their place here.

Here, there is a place for everyone. No one jostles for position. No one tries to squeeze in an imaginary hole. All who would come, all who seek, all who stand, all who surrender their lives have a place. It is a place for everyone to worship, love, strengthen, serve, and be served.

When they arrive, they are noticed – a quick glance from the faithful, a small smile, and a slight nod as everyone acknowledges the power of God in that place. Their place.

Each brings something new, a new gift for God. They come with their newness, their seeker's heart. They come with their situation. They come with their confidence, their pride, and their effort. They come with their shame, their disappointment, their rejection, their brokenness. They come with their circumstance.

They come and they stand, giving over the fullness of their beings to God.

Each is aware of the others, knowing and seeing their gifts and contributions. Each understands the role they have been called to. Each appreciates the roles that others have been called to fill. They are a friendship, and they are a family. They are brothers and sisters.

They are all geese.

As the people stand quietly, humbly, stilly in that place, that open place that always has enough room for one more, the Lord washes over them all in the magnificence of His fullness and His glory is revealed.

In the true community of God.

"So the people brought all of these things to the entrance of the Tabernacle... and the whole community came and stood there in the Lord's presence.... ... and the glorious presence of the Lord appeared to the whole community." - Leviticus 9:5,23b

5 | Follow the Leader

"Be very careful never to make treaties with the people in the land where you are going. If you do, you soon will be following their evil ways." - Exodus 34:12

God demands that we not make allegiances here on earth. He knows that the world will trick us into living in its ways and that if we are not careful, we will follow their path straight to destruction.

The world leads us as a tour guide would, walking backward to make sure we are following in every step, jumping through every hoop, maneuvering around every obstacle in exactly the way their leadership dictates. The world watches us make fools of ourselves as we labor to get it right, to take every step carefully and with the approval of those watching.

The path of the world is fraught with indulgence; it is an invitation to self.

It is an invitation to copy the world's leaders, their most successful or prominent or famous, by satisfying self, pursuing self, and protecting self.

We start forming our relationships physically, using sex to cement our hearts to one another to make up for the lack of a meaningful attraction. We use love as a weapon to manipulate one another into doing as we would prefer.

We make connections and sit through almost intolerable social events because that, and not our innate abilities or hard work, is what will move us up the career ladder.

We drive past the hitchhiker on the highway, walk past the pregnant teenager in the grocery store, roll up our windows when the homeless approach at a stoplight, turn our backs on individuals trapped in addiction, and drive miles out of our way to avoid the poorest, and therefore unsafe, areas of town because the world tells us that is not our path.

Self, self, self. There is no time, no money, no charity, no meaning for anyone else in the world.

We wouldn't want to be eliminated from the game for something so silly as not following directions.

Were we to stop, to commit ourselves to something different or take a new path, we would be shunned and excluded. The world would turn its back on us as it has so many others who do not play by their rules, and we could have no hope of rising to a position of respect, prominence, success, or leadership.

We believe that if we are good followers, someone somewhere might one day peg us as a good leader.

That is not to say such leadership comes easily. It is why the world watches so carefully each step we take, each obstacle we slink our way through. The world takes note of our obedience or lack thereof. When the time comes to take that next step, when the world tags us as a potential leader, our ability to follow comes back to testify either for or against us.

The slightest misstep, that moment we went off course, that time we followed our own passions and blazed our own paths, defines us as an outsider. It sets us apart from those who have spent their lives in the system, diligently working each step to make sure they were in line with the world's orders.

When we realize they will never choose us, that our detours, defiance or disobedience have undermined our leadership potential, even by this ridiculous definition, we cannot help but wonder who has been facing backward. The world has been leading blind, not knowing where it was going but insisting to arrive, but has it been leading us toward something or away from it?

Behind us stands another leader, the one the world has had its eye on from the beginning. He is a scraggly man, a loner, an outsider. He has made Himself that way by refusing to play by the world's rules, refusing to follow.

He stands watching with a simple sad look in His eyes. He is not making noise, not demanding that everyone turn around and look at Him. He mostly wanders, kicking a rock here and there and not a bit dismayed at being out of the game.

He wanted it that way.

His mere presence frees others to follow His example, to escape the pressured compliance of a treaty with the world, the silent agreement most of us have made to seek what the world is seeking, to obtain what it deems is good and valuable, to live the comfortable life of self that the in-crowd popularized, to follow.

And though He stands seemingly outside it all, His life is not purposeless. The absence of the pursuit of self is not the pursuit of nothing. It does not mean we excuse ourselves from the playground and stand idle all day.

This guy seems to have it figured out. He has removed Himself from the situation, and though He looks harmless enough, innate enough, sterile enough to many of us, there is something about the way He stands, the way He looks around, even the way His foot strikes the ground that screams something deeper is present. It screams purpose, even as it is silent in selflessness.

That is perhaps how He does it, how He has the resolve to stand on the outside. He is selfless, and not thinking of Himself frees Him from caring what anyone else thinks.

Our problem is that we do not seem to know who we are if we are not followers. If we cannot define our progress by where we are in this obstacle course we call the world, and if we step outside of the pursuit of self and give ourselves up, then who we are becomes this muddled mixture of in-betweenness where we know only what we no longer wish to be without having filled that empty space with new purpose.

His silent invitation and our restlessness lead us out of the world's conga line, looking for a new way. We search for new meaning, a new path to blaze. But we keep one eye on all we've given up to make sure life doesn't pass us by, to convince ourselves we are not missing anything while we know that all we have given up is keeping one eye on us, desperate for us to falter and fail.

Before we know it, our feet pass over a little pebble and that nagging imp in us that cannot leave these things alone decides to kick it a little ways, just as we saw the Man doing when He first caught our eye. We look up to see who is watching, who saw us dragging our feet and playing around.

Just the Man. He smiles in our direction. The world may have noticed, but to them it was inconsequential, the act of a lonely and meaningless nobody with a superiority complex who thinks they are too good for the games and the way it has worked for thousands of years.

He kicks another rock, and we follow suit. There is something about the quiet simplicity of His actions that makes us want what He has, that morphs us into another sort of follower. On some level, He knows that we are copying Him, beginning to follow His motions, but He is no tour guide. If we want to follow, He welcomes our discipleship, but His is not a leadership of control. He is not watching to make sure we do everything just right, laughing at our missteps and laughing at our mistakes that leave us fallen on our fannies in the mud.

His is a leadership of invitation, and it is His example that is most inviting. It was the simple act of His kicking a humble stone that made His way so enticing to us, that made us want to toe the dirt and rock the pebble from the ground ourselves. It is not His acts that call us to copy them but His manner of acting. It is His personality, His attitude, His presence that commands something more.

This invitation is in everything He does. He walks across uneven terrain without a flinch or a word. He climbs a tree to get a better view, not of the chaos but of the majesty around Him. Not as a gawking spectator but as a small piece of an unimaginable puzzle. He dances through the field because in the absence of self, He does not care who sees.

That is our invitation to dance. The first time, maybe it takes a moment for our feet to get the rhythm and for His invitation to break free our hearts, but it does not take long before we boogie in the bayou in reckless abandon.

When we realize what we are doing, we pause for a moment and remember what we left behind, knowing now that it has been so long since we looked back, since we tried to keep track of what we might have missed out on. It matters not.

Because we wouldn't give up this dance for anything in the world.

We follow a Man who isn't lording anything over us but instead calls to us with the simple invitation of His freedom.

The more we follow this Man, the more of these moments we share where life seems to melt away, and we no longer care who is watching. Maybe we even want the world to see us dance, but we are far beyond demanding their attention. We have adapted His leadership style, the style of selflessness that demonstrates something deeper than the world has ever seen and commands attention without demanding it.

His feet move in purpose, and ours follow without a thought. After sharing this dance, we would go anywhere with Him.

He moves fearlessly over rough terrain, through trials and briars and obstacles that would make anyone else pause for a second thought. He does not flinch, so neither do we, walking firmly but softly over the things that pose a threat to our very lives, the thorns that cut our feet or the vines that trip us up. Though they sting for a moment, the feeling is not enough to drive us back.

We will never turn back.

Our shoulders sag a bit, our bodies a little fatigued, but something more powerful calls us forward. We push on and hardly notice our energy falling because the strength of the One we follow is more potent. Ahead, we cannot see where He is going or why, but we know there will be something beautiful there.

Our legs burn with the effort of the climb, shallow but persistently uphill. This is the place where the world would be watching. They are pointing at something, laughing at what appears foolishness. We only notice them out of the corner of our eye. We don't even care any more.

Our eyes are forward, watching this Man who called us with His quiet strength, invited us simply to follow His example and give up what the world was asking of us and what it promised in return for the chance to be free.

Suddenly, He turns and we see the sweat pouring down His face for the first time. The thorns, which never cut our feet, have pierced His brow and blood mixes with His sweat. The sagging in our shoulders eases a little as a beam twice as tall as this Man rolls off and crashes to the ground with a thud.

This is Golgotha. This is where we understand what it means to have done as we have done, to have responded to the invitation to abandon self.

To follow.

Even to dance.

"'If any of you wants to be my follower,' he told them, 'you must put aside your selfish ambition, shoulder your cross, and follow me.'" - Mark 8:34b

6 | Four Square

"'Why are you frightened?' he asked. 'Why do you doubt who I am?'" - Luke 24:38

There is something in us that is slow to grow in faithfulness but quick to doubt. Doubt is most pernicious when we start to fear that God might not be who He claims. To spare our hearts the pain of hope, we give the world, other people, and even God just one chance – one short, limited chance – to respond as we see fit before we draw our own conclusions and take matters into our own hands.

The concept seems so simple. If we are who we think we are, and we have a pretty good idea just who that is, then we can readily predict who others are and their readiness to respond to our needs and requests. Because we are so adept at understanding our own position and painting ourselves into a box, we paint others into boxes. Including God.

God seems like the kind of deity who would be happy in a box. After all, He took thousands of years and dozens of writers and great care to tell us His story so we can know who He is and who He is not. He is loving, kind, gentle, always good, working on behalf of His children and this world. He is forgiving, gracious, wise, and wonderful. And He is so much more.

This attention to His character, spread throughout His word and confirmed through history, makes it too easy to put Him in a box. We readily expect God to be a constant force, never-changing, always responding as His character testifies.

When we face a hardship or trial, we expect Him to respond in strength.

When our burdens are too heavy, we expect Him to share the yoke.

When the questions are too big to ask, let alone answer, we expect Him to work it out.

When illness or financial hardship or relational difficulties arise, we expect Him to heal, to provide, to restore.

These are the character traits He's promised He holds. This is His heart, laid out in Scripture for us. This is the God of the Bible. This is what He's said He will do – strengthen, lighten, work, heal, provide, restore.

He has also said one other thing, which we often overlook – His ways are not our ways. They are higher.

Our problem, and the place we leave open for God to fail us, is that we embrace the wrong definitions of His goodness. We may not know the details or exactly what's happening, and we may admit we don't have the answers, but we at least have a fairly good idea what those answers should look like.

We serve up the ball in a cutthroat game of four square. It would simplify our lives for everyone to stay in their box, to play their position, but we are almost as eager to mark down a point against them when they fail to counter our serve.

His response should be instantaneous and final, regardless of the situation, we say. His strength should crush our hardship with one definitive blow. Anything less is our point.

His yoke should be uneven so we can shift our way out from underneath our burden altogether and leave Him to carry it. Anything less is our point.

When He works out our biggest problems or answers our biggest questions, the result ought to be instant peace or promotion or success or reward. Anything less is our point.

His healing should wipe out all disease and put us in shape to run a marathon. Anything less is our point.

His provision must be more than enough food to eat, cable television, high speed internet, a flashy car, new clothes, an unlimited cell phone plan, and maybe a new coat of paint on the house. Anything less is our point.

His intervention in our relationships should remind everyone why we are the wisest, why we are right, and send them crawling back to us in apology and affirming our superiority. Anything less is our point.

So we rack up points against Him, and yes, we're keeping track. We serve point after point, believing that like any good player, He will respond in one bounce. One opportunity is all it should take for a God like our God to fix everything. As soon as that ball bounces twice, we chalk up another point and hold it against Him. Like little children on the playground, we loudly declare the score at every turn and taunt Him to start putting His own points on the board.

As long as He scores against the world. As long as He doesn't put up points at our expense.

What we want is not for God to beat us, to go all-out spiking that ball in every box He can find, every box we've created, but for Him to score only against the world. To score some of the same points we're looking to tally up so that at the very least, we can say that God is a formidable player. Perhaps even an ally.

Any formidable player on the court is an asset. Someone, anyone, defending another box gives us permission to stay out of there. We can stay contently in our own corner of the world, the box we've drawn around ourselves.

Life gets tricky when we have to change boxes. What used to be left might now be straight across or right or some other disorienting position that requires us to change our automated responses.

Shift one box and suddenly, that trained spike to the left does no good. There's no box there, no opponent to counter our move.

The sun in the new box shines differently, coming in at a different angle or beating against our backs.

The wind blows from a different direction.

The scenery is different, more distracting.

No, it is much simpler for everyone to stay in their box and play admirably.

Though nobody ever said we're committed to making things simple.

We are anxious to jump in and take over someone else's position when it seems, to us, that they aren't defending well. God isn't answering our prayers like a magic genie, which means He's out to lunch or just not as skilled a player as we once assumed.

No problem, though; we can be God.

We can find our own strength, our own force, our own healing or restoration or provision. We can make it on our own, and now that we know God isn't in the business of answering our serve, we take that as the go-ahead that He's calling us to self-sufficiency.

While we're defending His box, He takes over ours. That's how the game works; that's where we put Him. We are the king player, the four square, and now He is the one – the lowest on the totem pole, the poorest competitor. We hope that He'll be able to handle the little things, the things we used to be responsible for, while we're tackling the bigger issues.

For awhile, we make a pretty good god. We are able to gift ourselves, through whatever means, with the objects of our desire. That next rung on the corporate ladder. That new relationship that we know will lead to marriage. That refund from the utility company that will pay for the unexpected car trouble. Those things that God neglected to do for us even while we continued begging Him to defend His position.

Before we found out He must not be the player we thought He was; He must be a different kind of God.

We soon realize that we aren't the player we thought we were, either. Yes, for a short time, we satisfied ourselves and played the role of God to a T, defending His box and sometimes raising it as a testimony to the power of the will. Occasionally, we'll even thank Him for the gift He's given us – the gift of godness, the power and skill that enabled us to pull it off.

But it doesn't last. We quickly grow weary of being the most powerful player, of trying to rule the court and control everything in it. We feel the pressure of our high profile, knowing that if we blink at just the wrong second, it could all be for nothing. We can fall as quickly as we rose.

Now, everyone is serving against us, trying to rack up points. God, the world, the enemy – they set their sights on us.

One momentary lapse of concentration, and the whole thing falls apart. That is the diligence required by God, required of us now that we are standing in His box, playing His position.

And it's not even satisfying, not as time wears on. Not as the pressure starts to get to us. Not as the beads of sweat roll into our eyes, and we can't whisk them away. Our hands must stay free to defend; our vision must stay focused. Not as we realize it is all for nothing anyway.

Once we learn to play God in our lives, we realize we lack the proper wisdom. We cannot answer all of the players at once. We cannot answer one player all of the time. If the playground count is accurate, we are the only players not racking up points.

That is when God serves a tough shot, the one that eludes us on the first bounce and forces our resignation of the four square. The ball bounces in our box, but we are powerless to field it. A diving attempt to save the point, to protect our new status, to continue ruling the court leaves us face-first on the blacktop at the feet of the One square.

He resumes His position, playing again as the four square. The box is the same, but He is comfortable there. It is a box that holds Him to His promises – of goodness, faithfulness, integrity, and tender mercy. He doesn't mind when we expect those things of Him.

From our old box in our new perspective, we see the game with new eyes. We see the way He plays it.

Sometimes, God intercepts our serve and sends it sailing toward the world, using His community to answer our cries. The world is not required to answer us directly, either. Maybe they send that ball back to God... or maybe toward the enemy. In the midst of the game, our answer gets lost. Not because God isn't deserving of the four square but because those that often come between us are playing the game, too.

The ball doesn't stay bouncing in God's box while we wait on His response; it bounces all over the court.

We look down and are humbled by our own box. Not the four square box of God but the one square box of man. And we realize we were right all along.

It is better for everyone to stay in their own box.

"As you yourself have said, 'God is greater than any person.' So why are you bringing a charge against Him? You say, 'He does not respond....' But God speaks again and again..."- Job 33:12b-14

7 | Freeze Tag

"People can never predict when hard times might come. Like fish in a net or birds in a snare, people are often caught by sudden tragedy." - Ecclesiastes 9:12

Oh, how we would love to predict when hard times will come. Some of the prophets received a little insight: God told them when a famine would come and for how many years (or what indeterminate length of time) the lands would lay barren. They were able to go to the people and proclaim the coming struggle, then pile the storehouses full enough to tide Israel over until better times prevailed.

We would like that kind of advanced notice, that direct word from God that tells us when something bad is coming, what it will be, and how long it will last. If there's something we can do to end our suffering sooner, just tell us, Lord! In the meantime, we pile our storehouses full of whatever we think might tide us through our worst nightmares.

Despite our built-up prayers, funds, material resources, food and water (always necessary in case of emergency), plans B and C and D, tragedy still comes when we least expect it, when we feel less than adequately prepared, and stops us in our tracks.

Stops us dead.

Because when tragedy strikes, it is the furthest thing on our mind. We are just moving along, pursuing our passions and advancing our place in the world. Life is a cruise, or maybe a joy ride, and we would like to believe that tragedy can never come when things are going so well.

Especially when our storehouses are full.

Then, all of a sudden, we're singled out. Like some other-worldly (or under-worldly) influence decided to lift just one finger and strike us down. Individually. Selected out of the billions of people who walk the earth, this disaster comes hand-picked upon us.

Not everyone battles cancer, and many who do survive many decades. Why, then, does the doctor have to share those scary words like "advanced stages" and "inoperable" on our phone?

Not everyone who has a child wants one, and many more are poor or worse, abusive, parents. Why, then, do one loving husband and wife struggle to conceive?

Not everyone had rainwater pouring into their basement, so why are we stuck wading through several feet of water to unplug the dryer and try to save as many family heirlooms as possible?

These are the things that stop us in our tracks not only because they are such overwhelming events but because they run counter to everything we thought we had, everything we were working toward. Our energies have to be redirected, and so powerfully so that we have to give up our pursuit of everything else to clean up the mess life has thrown at us.

We feel cursed, specially chosen and favored not by God but by some other force, our enemy. Here we've been gleefully skipping around life's playground, where the grass is green and little flowers dot the fields, and out of nowhere, Satan tags us with this. Not the slower, weaker runners or the social outcasts or the kid who has already tripped over his own shoelaces.

No, Satan has come after us. He's tagged us, frozen us in this place of despair and misery, stopped us in the middle of the playground. And now, we're left standing there, unable to move by the rules of the game.

We can only now wait on the forces of freedom to unfreeze us.

That is our prayer, is it not? For someone unfrozen to come and free us. That is where we find our hope.

Unfrozen is the doctor testing a new treatment with promising results who has finally returned our call and agreed to meet with us.

It is the miracle of modern science that overcomes infertility and births our own child in our arms.

It is the appearance of neighbors we never met who flock over in their waders to help us save our home.

It is these big things, and the little ones as well, that give us that second to blink and focus on new hope. Once we feel ourselves starting to thaw, we are able to run again.

The first place we run is our storehouse, our "base," where we're supposed to be free from further taggings. It is our place of retreat where the enemy can neither find nor catch us, and we have supplied it with our absolute best to ensure our preservation until the game is over.

When we pull open the doors and lay our hands on all of the stuff we accumulated for these difficult times, we are disappointed.

The thousands of prayers we prayed for God to keep us from disaster don't apply now, and they are so old that even their echoes have long faded out. The silence humbles us; we know we cannot store prayers.

The food we planned to eat, the Word of God that nourishes us, does not speak to this disaster. The verses we chose and built our lives around, the ones that always gave us so much hope and anticipation, actually anger us in this moment. These are not the messages of the Lord we need to hear right now! We're surrounded by sugar cubes when we need a big, fat steak.

The reserves of water have all but evaporated, waiting so long here for us to come. It was supposed to be life-giving, living water to quench our thirst and hydrate our bodies. But the Jesus we created and bottled for emergencies just is not the Jesus we need right now.

The wood we stashed to build fire is rotten through and through, crumbling to dust and ash even in the absence of flame.

Then, the enemy peeks his head through the door and just as we turn to look, he tags us again.

No fair! we cry. I'm on base! I'm safe!

He looks around and laughs. "This isn't base," he replies, and we know he is right.

Nothing here is preserving. Nothing here is life-giving. Nothing is even as we expected it to be. From a distance, when the game first began, we looked at our storehouse as the perfect base. But now inside, needing shelter and comfort and provision, we see how old, rotten, and spoiled our wares are and we have to start looking around for somewhere new to call home.

Somewhere new to seek safety.

As soon as someone unfreezes us again. Because now, we are stuck in the darkness of our molded storehouse. The same bugs that ate our food are nibbling at our hearts. Through the small crack between the ajar door and its jamb, we keep one eye open for any sign of help. The first person we see who is not the enemy, we will cry out and beg them to come and unfreeze us.

We feel that freeing touch, then spring out the door like a rocket, looking around frantically for the true base, the one agreed-upon.

It is not too hard to spot. The true base is not a where or a what, but a Who. It is Christ, Who has promised to be our refuge. Enemy, luck, pure chance, or the laws of nature – no matter who is "It," all have to respect the security of Christ.

There, we find in richness and great bounty all of the sustaining supplies we tucked away in our own storehouse too long ago to remember.

There is the food that feeds us, body and soul. It is the bread of His body and the vine of His blood. It is the hearty main course of His word, spread before us like a veritable buffet with all the trimmings and a dish for every taste, a message for every tragedy.

There is the living water of Christ Himself. Drinking of His goodness soothes our throat and moistens our tongue. We can swallow more easily whatever life hands us, knowing that even so, we will never be thirsty again.

There is the wood of the cross, preserved perfectly thousands of years later. It is wood good enough to kindle a fire, setting our hearts ablaze with the passion of God.

It is there, in Christ, where our prayers echo ceaselessly, where they are never forgotten.

Of course this is our perfect base! Of course this is the place of safety and refuge! Our faded old storehouse on the far horizon of the playground was nothing more than our failed attempt at this, at Christ. This place makes much more sense – and here, there is no darkness, no mold, no stench or moisture or moths that kill and destroy.

Christ is the perfect shelter.

We would fool ourselves to say the enemy cannot touch us here. He dances around the base, taunting and teasing and poking at us with his fingers. But here in Christ's shadow, after the enemy's touch, we are not frozen. Here, he cannot strike us to stop us in our tracks.

We are on base, we tell him. We are in the sanctuary of Christ, the place on the playground where your game doesn't work.

The enemy dances a little more, then runs off in pursuit of easier targets, those who aren't clinging to home base under the protection of Jesus. He checks back every now and again to see if we have been stupid enough to leave, but with all the provision in the world under His fingernail, where else would we go?

As we nestle into home base and settle in for the long haul, content to never run again, we look up at Christ tending His flock as a shepherd, herding those who have come to Him for rest and security. Those who are taking a break from the game, who are now milling around in His pasture pursuing again their passions.

He inches His way closer, slowly but deliberately, trying to throw us off and convince us that He's not up to anything. He stops here and there to pick a flower or kick a clod of dirt, looking away when He catches us watching.

When at last He is within reach, He stretches out one finger and touches our hearts.

The fullness of His power stops us dead in our tracks. We are frozen again, this time speechless and in awe – of His beauty, mercy, grace, power, bounty, love, and tender care. We are overwhelmed with beauty in particular, and profoundly with grace. We are humbled there in that moment, the stark contrast of what we know of ourselves now competing with this holy stillness.

We look up to see a sheepish smile cross our Savior's face. He knows we are stricken, not by His finger but by the Presence. He knows we are stunned, frozen in this moment. He knows we are a little afraid to ask, sensing the holiness and not wanting to ruin or sacrifice the moment.

So His eyes meet ours for a brief second, and with two simple words, He answers the question we hesitate to ask:

"I'm It."

"Listen...; stop and consider the wonderful miracles of God!" - Job 37:14

8 | The Ground Is Lava

"Deeper and deeper I sink into the mire; I can't find a foothold to stand on." - Psalm 69:2a

One of the toughest challenges of living in our fallen, hectic world is that nothing stays the same for long. We hold on to what we have until what we have becomes obsolete… or worse. It is tough to figure out from one day to the next just what we've got or what it means.

Yesterday's status symbol is today's polluter.

Yesterday's sound investment is today's stock market disaster.

Yesterday's perfect family is today's public apology.

Our dreams, goals, must-haves and rather-nots ebb and flow as the ocean. We have trouble finding even one steady foothold. As soon as we find one small piece of solid ground to stand on, suddenly, we can't move. Something is pulling us down. We look to see the ground, the mud, the muck covering up the tops of our sneakers. Something burns and the smell of that place offends our nose. Our lungs struggle for clean air. The heat shoots up our legs.

That foothold shifts out from under us, and we're sinking fast.

The ground is lava.

Life's playground is a place where any surface can turn to lava at a moment's notice. Carpet, grass, gravel, pavement – these are just a word away from turning molten and burning us alive. All it takes is one mischievous little imp with a loud voice:

"The ground is lava!"

Okay, so it takes a mischievous little imp with a lot of charisma. Because as we all know, there are two appropriate reactions to this invitation to play on an imaginary volcano. First, we can shoot the imp a look of disbelief and unconcern that says, "The ground is the ground."

Second, we can run as fast as possible.

There's something about the running, isn't there? Something drives us to play the game, whether anyone else knows we're in it or not. If we stood in the middle of the field long enough, someone would clue us in and tell us we're melting. And if we ran to higher ground, there is a chance that nobody intended we play the game at all, and they wouldn't tell us when it's safe to step down.

Still, we play. Better safe than sorry.

It is this instinct that teaches us to jump ship, to scurry and scramble for something solid at the slightest sign of trouble. The ground cracks open, and we're about to stand toe-to-toe with the core of life as we know it – with the heat and the tar and the steam and the muck and the shadows we've built our reputations on. Our lives are about to light, and we start to panic.

Is there any ground left that isn't lava? Is there anywhere to go, anything to do, to escape the shifting ground? Are we confident to stand... or shaken to run?

There's something we neglect to notice in our lava experiences. It's not that the ground is falling out beneath us or that the steam burns our eyes. It's not the deep rumbling that deafens, dizzies, and disorients us, though a great deal could be said about this seismic activity. Our problem is that in our frantic rush to find new footing, we overlook where we already stand:

On the mountain.

Lava is not a factor in the grazing fields of the cattle or the third floor office or the suburban homestead. It's not got a place in the busy streets of a sprawling metropolis or the vast sands of the Sahara. When the San Francisco landscape burst open during the great quake of 1906, no lava spewed forth to swallow the city.

No, lava is strictly a volcanic experience – a volatile mountain marvel.

That is how it always strikes us, as well. We feel ourselves gaining confidence, growing in faith, exercising our trust. We're on our way up the mountain, climbing higher and higher with each sure-footed step. Then, that rumble hits. The ground shakes beneath us.

We instinctually forget every solid step that led us here, every inch of growth and success, every speck of strength. Doubt settles in as we grow keenly aware of the sweat and the steam, the stench of sulfur, the strain in our legs.

Why were we climbing this mountain again?

The summit glows orange with a steady stream of molten disappointment. It seems to fade into the distance as the temperature rises and heat hazes our eyes. We feel foolish for having aspired to that summit in the first place. We'd thought it was something beautiful, something safe and glorious and majestic.

Now, it doesn't look so glorious.

Our one-time goal looks more and more like a pipe dream. Lava peeks through the surface of the mountain, covering our footprints, which only moments ago felt so sure, so solid.

I knew it! we think. I knew I was just floating on air, high on life, deluding myself into thinking this was worth it, that it was even working. I just knew it!

Oh, we are so very foolish. Not to have attempted the climb. No, for the summit is just as grand as it has always been, and the mountain as sure. We are foolish for letting our eyes deceive us, for being taken in by the harsh sight of that lava that seems to cover all.

The flow is powerful and sudden. A few more seconds, and the mountain will be swallowed whole, we think. Every piece broken apart and rushing downward in a river of fire and heat and sulfur. Soon, the whole mountain will glow orange around us, and we will stand as only a shadow, to be seen from a distance but never rescued. No one is coming after us here.

We are utterly alone, desperately isolated while the ground liquefies and draws us into its traps.

If only we could gather our wits about us for one minute, for one measly look at the truth. Then, we would see that the mountain is still just a mountain and that this lava, while impressive in its size and strength, only spews forth from the most vulnerable places – the cracks that already existed, the craters as old as the earth itself. And the lava flows downward not so willy-nilly but in ruts and routes well-worn by nature and previous eruptions.

This lava is almost... almost predictable.

There are solid places left on the mountain, steady footholds to get us to the top. It's just that panic that keeps us from seeing them because too often, we're caught on those vulnerable places or stuck in a rut.

That is how our enemy, the master of fire and brimstone, likes it. He's not going to send the powers of Hell after us until he sees the cracks forming, until he thinks we're trapped. That is his dirty little game to keep us from the summit, to shake our faith at precisely the right moment to send us scurrying for safety – away from the lava, far from the mountain.

But God seizes these moments, too.

He stills us and demands we not be shaken, no matter how the earth trembles beneath our feet. He pleads with us to look around, to notice the mountain and the all-too-well-timed eruption. When we do, we see what He sees – we are so close to the top with no reason to stop now.

One small step to the left or the right will set us on a new path, free from the flow of destruction and disappointment. A quick turn of our head will shield our breath from the bitter stench and allow clean air to enter our lungs. We catch a second wind for our final push, and we find the strength to strain against the powerful force that shakes us to the core.

Then, God stops us once more. "Look down," He says. "Look beneath your feet on the ground where you now stand. Do you realize what's happened here?"

We don't. We are clueless to what God is getting at. This side of the mountain, this new place we're standing, is just like the rest of it. Just as hard-formed and solid as our rut or the place a few steps away that cracked under us.

Slowly, an idea forms in our mind. Suddenly, we see what He was trying to tell us.

This mountain, this entire mountain, was formed by the lava itself. Eruption after eruption, year after year, century after century, fire and brimstone chased man off this mountain. Ourselves included. And each time, when the earth stilled and the magma cooled, a new surface formed – a hard, solid surface that became the foothold for those who dare to climb.

This is holy ground, tried and tested and true ground formed by our tribulations, victories, and failures. This place is nothing new; it is the very place where we have been tested over and over and over again. Each granule of rock represents a former vulnerability, a place once cracked open and flowing with lava.

The enemy never counted on that; he never stopped to think that his greatest attacks would form our strength. His successes at scaring us, at forcing our descent, have strengthened our journey on this mountain. Though he brought fire and sulfur and heat, he did not have the stamina to maintain it forever. When his resolve failed and he abandoned the mountain, the lava cooled and our strength was just beginning.

Once, there were weaknesses where we now set our feet. There were cracks and holes and ruts that allowed the lava to chase us away. Now, we rejoice in our former weaknesses because they have become our strength.

His strength. At precisely the moment we're exposed, God is already at work redeeming and cooling the situation. He is already sealing the cracks and filling in the ruts so that His strength shows in our path.

Why are we so quick to run when the earth starts shaking? Why do we let ourselves tremble or let the fumes choke us? Do we not have it in us to look around and take notice, to understand the building work that God is doing through the seeming attack of our mortal enemy?

We stand triumphantly on a mountain formed by our own weaknesses, by the exploitation and redemption of our deepest vulnerabilities. Heat and fire from the core of our existence expand and erupt, then cool and contract to form holy ground. On that holy ground, we carefully place our feet and strive for the summit, for that mountaintop experience. There, at the top, an all-consuming and sanctifying fire dwells that sets our hearts ablaze with new passion as it billows into the Heavens.

Rather than hazing our eyes, this fire renews them, and we see with great clarity the work of God stretching out to the horizons. His breath rustling the leaves on each tree. His hand guiding the rivers that bring life to the landscape. His light shining in the sun.

We hazard to look down the mountain, lava still flowing from a crack here and there, and cannot comprehend how far He's brought us, how high we are lifted up. His strength, grace, and mercy built that mountain out of our much lesser things – fear, panic, weakness, vulnerability.

It is awe, not brimstone, that takes our breath away.

"Now I stand on solid ground, and I will publicly praise the Lord." - Psalm 26:12

9 | Hide and Seek

"...they heard the Lord God walking about in the garden, so they hid themselves among the trees. The Lord God called to Adam, 'Where are you?'" – Genesis 3:8-9

As beautiful as the idea of an all-knowing and still all-loving God is, there are some things we wish He didn't know about us. We are eager to show Him our accomplishments, to hold up a gold star for this or that achievement, but we would rather not acknowledge our shortcomings.

We know never to hide the light of God in our lives under a bushel, but once we sense our candle has already gone out, we have no trouble turning a basket over our heads and trying to lay low for awhile.

Our relational God plays along for a bit, stomping around in the garden around us and hoping we will come out and own up to whatever we have done.

Let us not delude ourselves – He knew precisely where Adam and Eve were, and He knows where we are, too.

But He wants us to show Him, to reveal ourselves and tell Him all about it.

That is difficult: we would rather not reveal ourselves. That was Adam and Eve's problem. When they spoke and reached out to the Lord, so close that they heard His footsteps, they did not reveal themselves right away.

Instead, they answered simply. Yes, Lord. We heard you, but we were naked, so we hid.

It was their nakedness, not their wrongdoing that sent them scurrying into the bushes at the sound of an approaching friend. They were not hiding from a vengeful, spiteful God who they believed would punish them with eternal Hell or worse. It was their guilt, their shame that sent them running. They felt exposed, and they preferred God not to see them like this.

Somewhere, we have gotten the idea that God shouldn't see the worst of us, that we should take ourselves outside of His camp until our impurity wears off. We dive headfirst into the bush and take cover to hide our iniquities and our nakedness. When He calls out to us, we still answer. Just please, Lord, don't make us get out of the bush.

Not until we're covered. Not until we finish beating ourselves up sufficiently over our shortcomings. Not until we are dirty and scratched and bleeding from the thorns here. Or at least close Your eyes until we can run down to the river and hide ourselves there in something cleansing.

The current, we tell Him, and the natural flow of life will make us willing to show ourselves again, when we can admit what we have done and feel no shame.

So we hide from God in the midst of the world, waiting on things to clear up before we step back out, expecting everything to work itself out and time to heal all wounds. Time. In the bush, we have plenty of it and we watch our bodies scar over, growing hard in the wounded areas. We take hold of the leaves and weave together linens for ourselves, something makeshift to hide our nakedness.

No wonder so many of us are walking around hardened, clothed in the undergrowth of this world! Too many of us believe that in covering our shame with whatever is handy, even thorny or dried up leaves, we have made ourselves more presentable to and worthy of God. We want to pop out of the bush and start walking with Him again like nothing is all that different.

But He knows something is wrong; He senses the rash spreading beneath our new coverings, that tender spot becoming more sensitive by the moment that refuses to be hardened, refuses to heal. It is kept alive by the darkness and by the toxin that permeates our handmade clothing, our home remedy.

This is why when we come to God in earnest, repent and turn our hearts toward Him, the first thing He does is demand a change of wardrobe. He doesn't want us clothed in the chafing clothes of the world, the ones we knit together ourselves in hiding; He wants us clothed in righteousness, a breathable fabric perfectly designed and tailored to us.

After we have stepped forward and answered His first question of "Where are you," though He knew the answer all along and was only waiting on our reply, He poses a more pressing query: Who told you that you were naked?

Nowhere prior to the eating of one deliciously bad apple does God, the serpent, or either human mention anything about nakedness being a bad thing. God did not set man's foot on solid ground and declare, "Go forth and multiply... and hide your shame!" Yet with all of the knowledge of good and evil, Adam and Eve instinctually looked down and began to blush.

Their nakedness, no different than it had been a few moments ago, was not suddenly disgusting or embarrassing; it was their knowledge that had changed. They understood the vulnerability of nakedness, the way that their most tender and exposed areas could come in contact with, and be harmed by, nearly anything.

Poison ivy, anyone?

With the juice still dribbling off their chins, they realized the delicate situation they were in. Perhaps they were already scratched, already bruised. Maybe their bodies were dirty from tending the garden. Maybe they drew a stark contrast between the condition of their beings and the being of God, who they had seen face-to-face every day of their lives.

They had felt no pain, so how could they have known the damage that was coming upon them? They knew well, we can assume, the body's innate wisdom to heal itself; there were no bandages in the garden, no ice packs or hot water bottles. Is it possible their shame was not as we think of it, was not anatomical, not some giggly realization of male and female?

It is possible their shame came in understanding the delicacy of their own bodies and the way they had taken that for granted, the way they had done whatever they pleased without a thought to potential hazards. Could they have suddenly become burdened with the idea that God was taking such good care of them, protecting even their physical bodies and tirelessly healing them without a word?

Maybe their shame was as ours often is – the shame of realizing how utterly dependent upon God we are, then weighing ourselves down with the burden of being a burden and feeling entirely unworthy of His constant protection and care. They looked down and saw not male- and femaleness, but the normal wear and tear of the body and were ashamed by their carelessness and rebellion with God's design.

So they ducked behind a tree and prayed their makeshift clothing would hide their dirty little secrets. All the knowledge in the world told them they were naked, to answer God's second question, but they seemed to draw their own conclusions about what that meant. Maybe for a split second, through the knowledge of God's eyes, they saw as He saw and understood the beauty of their utter dependence, but their disobedience introduced sin at the same moment it opened their eyes, and sin introduced doubt, and doubt sent them taking headers into the bushes.

God's understanding of nakedness is quite different. He is not ashamed by the way He made us, and He is not burdened by being our God. If His plan had been to create self-sufficient people who merely enjoyed hanging out with Him and never needed guidance or protection or healing or discipline, then He would have been content to stop creation at five days. But God always wanted to be a God, a God over more than light and darkness or angels and demons. What He wanted, what the God of the Universe longed for most, was a people – a people who would recognize His presence and upon whom He could pour out His love.

He does not resent protecting us, healing us, loving us, saving us. He does not shudder at the wear and tear this world puts on our bodies; after all, it was He who created the thorn with the rose, the stone with the sand, the rain with the clouds. And it was He who created man with a soft skin, not one impervious to the rest of His creation.

He planned to be our God, just as He planned for us to be His people. He even planted an apple tree, knowing that one day, we might eat of it and know just how blessed a God He is to us. Knowing His goodness, we would surely run to Him and hold on tighter to this Lord.

But we ate too quickly, without His wisdom in our minds, and unleashed the power of sin and doubt to swirl through the leaves. Instead of doing as we had always done, though we were unaware, and hiding in Him to shield us from the world, we turned and ran into the world to hide from Him.

He knows just where we are, but He asks anyway, pleading with us to come out and run to Him. Being our loving God means He will never drag us, kicking and screaming, out of our hiding place, but He will stand just on the other side, casting a shadow and tapping His toe until we know we cannot breathe without His knowing it. Then, we will know that was the case all along.

We will realize that though we wanted not to be seen in our shame and in our nakedness, He saw us anyway. His approaching footsteps were not one of a seeker, but one of a Father who knows where His child's favorite hiding spot is but plays along anyway.

We will scratch the growing burning feeling beneath our worldly clothes and not try to hide the itch. And as we draw near to the God who always knew where we were, we will not be ashamed as He strips those clothes off our backs and tends to our tattered, beaten, bruised, and dirty flesh. He will carefully untangle the twigs from our matted hair. This, we will know with a sigh of relief, is what it means to be God's people.

We will watch with the tears of redemption in our eyes as He sews each stitch by hand in our new clothing, not made of scraps of the world but of the flesh of sacrifice that would be pleasing to Him.

As we watch our bodies heal, not with the hard calluses of open air and the mending of time but under the hands of the Great Physician, we will find a new place to hide.

It will be our place to hide away from the world, away from the sticks and the leaves and the dirt; it will be our place of refuge, with a roof over our heads and walls to shield us from the wind and the rain. There, the knowledge of the apple will do as it was intended and draw us closer to the God who yearns to be our God. There, there is no shame in nakedness, for we are cared for and tended to with the greatest love and gentleness. There, we are covered in grace and mercy, forever presentable to stand in front of the Lord and unconcerned with the opinion of anyone else.

This time, the world will be looking for us. It will be a place where we are never really hiding because we are never afraid of being found.

Anyone is welcome to seek us there.

"'But why did you need to search? ... You should have known that I would be in my Father's house.'"–Luke 2:49

10 | Hopscotch

"But Moses again pleaded, 'Lord, please! Send someone else!'" – Exodus 4:13

There are some places in this world that we are reluctant, if not outright unwilling, to go. Sometimes, our reason is obvious – the place is too remote, too violent, too desolate, or too far outside our comfort zone. In other cases, we hold our reasons close to our hearts and shake our heads like defiant toddlers.

No, Lord, we say. Not there.

Because there are some places that simply don't fit our concept of the course our lives should take. These are not just physical places; they are also areas of sacrifice or service or humility that we would prefer not to incorporate in our path.

It is not a path made by our own hands; this is the plan God laid out, the one He ordained for us before we were knit together in the womb. Before we knew there was even a playground, God was here laying out and numbering our steps that would lead us Home. And we were drawn to its uniformity, its consistency, and its seeming simplicity.

We wanted to know what He had for us.

The concept seemed simple enough: follow each step by number, and the path will lead us to Him. One step at a time, with plenty of space to steady ourselves before moving on to the next. Stay on the path, stay in the lines, plant each foot firmly, and this will be a smooth journey.

But something about the obvious path makes us cringe. We detest the idea of being a robot, of feeling like we live by rote. Thoughts of the Stepford Disciples or any of a number of seemingly-brainwashed "Christians," who believe that following God means living in denial of reality, fill our minds. We want to be engaged here, to have a say in our own progress, and to control our own destiny. And we shudder to think we can only be followers.

We feel like it is cheating to take the easy way, that life should not be a cakewalk. We decide to challenge ourselves by putting obstacles in our path. Namely one big rock that we throw toward the ground. We cast a stone on a place we're unwilling to go. Whatever step that stone blocks out, we will skip and move straight on to the next.

We love the idea of skipping a step here and there. That is how we get ahead in the world. We know because we have watched many before us win the game of life by doing this very thing – going a short distance, then skipping ahead by a step or two.

The rock lands just where we hoped it would, and our confidence soars; this should be simple enough to avoid. We try not to let on how thrilled we are at the idea of skipping right over that one.

That step seemed like a detour, completely out of line with the way we would design our lives. It would have been a distraction and could have thrown us off-course altogether. We are much more likely to succeed now, having avoided that obvious trap. We will pray for that place, but we will not go there.

God never would have ordained that for us, we think. It is completely out of character, requires a personality style or a giftedness that we don't see in ourselves. It was one of those places that was side-by-side with another that makes more sense, almost perfect sense maybe. By avoiding it, we actually straighten our path, and isn't the road to God both straight and narrow?

We study the new path. Each step is specifically proportioned to ensure we can set only one foot there; there is not room for two. This is going to require a certain skill and a little finesse.

We jump forward, anxious to begin. Our foot lands squarely in the first step, but we waste no time. Glory awaits. That perfect life of ease and prestige, the end of striving and the start of sainthood. We move quickly on to the second step, then the third before our speed gets the better of us and we tumble to the ground, stretching out one hand to break our fall.

Scraped knees and bloody palm later, we stand again. Our fall was nothing more than a misplaced foot, an unsteady landing. We focus our energies in our sole and begin once more, stepping here and then there and then driving forward again before our footing fails and sends us crashing back down.

More scrapes. More cuts. More blood. Little bits of rock and gravel stick out of our skin. We brush away the dirt, wipe a little spit on our wounds, and stare down the path.

The third time is the charm, we chant as we resolve to approach this task with more diligence, stronger attention. We watch our foot land in square one, watch the outline of our flesh all but fill the space, and use the power of our mind to lock that foot in place. We lift our foot to make the short leap to the next place, our eyes locked on that number two.

Solid there, we sneak a peek forward to the place we have blocked out, the one we don't have to touch or to visit, the one we determined to never set foot in. Minding that block out of the corner of our eye, we land not on the next step but somewhere in between, right on the line between where we were and where we were going. This place is nowhere, and it doesn't count.

These failed attempts have shown us the beauty of God's cartography. By mapping each step at just such a size, by ensuring we can place only one steady foot on the ground, He has guaranteed that our progress can come only through the delicate interplay of balance and motion. We must learn to steady ourselves while always moving forward. Failure at either ensures our fall.

With that in mind, we set about our path more patiently, more diligently. We take the time to find our balance but do not wait lest our knee begin to shake. And we make it further than ever before. One more step and we will land next to our rock, the block we have put in our path to cover the place we dare not go.

On our right foot, we attempt to move to the place that is left, but this crisscross motion attacks our balance. It threatens our uprightness. And then, it steals both and sends us right back to the ground.

Again and again, though we stand on our right foot, we cannot make the leap to what is left, what we have preserved next to the place we are unwilling to go. We eye the rock and see it more now as a stumbling block than an asset, but fear keeps us from moving it.

What if we were to go there? That place is still outside our comfort zone, still desolate and foreign and demanding. It requires more of us than we know of ourselves or are even sure we can offer.

Our efforts continue to fail, each time falling harder in our attempt to stay right in what is left. One flailing arm, futilely trying to save us from the harsh impact, knocks the stone out of the way and opens again this step in our path. This step that now taunts us, glaringly open and obviously numbered.

Whatever this is, this place is next. It will embrace and empower our feet, strengthen our balance, and serve as a launching point for whatever follows. We know we have avoided it too long, maybe missed out on something God wanted to offer us. All because we wanted to block this out, to cast a stone against this place and save ourselves from having to go there.

This place, by its very nature, requires commitment. It requires that we put both feet down, forcing ourselves to stop. But it's tough to think of staying there for any length of time.

The next time we approach, we plant both feet firmly, side-by-side. We neither fall nor fear the unknown. Because He has seen fit to provide our balance by opening our presence to something known, something comfortable we never questioned, while asking us to also step out, we know we will thrive here. We know we will gather whatever He planned by touching this place.

And this place, it is almost a place of rest. There is no fighting against the weight of our own bodies, no pressure to move any faster than we would so choose. Indeed, there is great work to be done here, and it is work that not only fulfills God's next step in our lives but refreshes and rejuvenates us.

Were it not for the coming steps, the future places, still calling out to us, we might be content to stay here forever.

As good as God has made this place, how much more of His goodness does the future hold? We want to keep journeying, to move and pursue that place called Home.

We must go again and set out on the right foot, landing square in the next place and holding our balance before moving forward once more. We savor each step, thankful that He ordained this specifically for us, thankful for the gift of having known each place. But we cannot help but look back.

We look back to that place we were most afraid to go, the one that did not seem to fit our personality or our lifestyle at all. Over our shoulder, we glance back and remember the lessons we learned there and the good work we set in motion, not only in our lives but in the lives of God's people because we repented and agreed to go where God called us.

This place where we never thought He would call us, this place where we were most unwilling to take ourselves, this place we never thought we could ever fit in nor impact, was the most precious place He ever chose for us.

Our stumbling block lay just off course, but still within reach. We let our foot roll over it, playing with it a little, tossing it back and forth while realizing the power we almost gave it in our lives. This little stone almost took God's precious gift because we let it hold that place, we gave it that power.

It rolls right again, just out of reach this time, and comes to land on the place we last left it – that invaluable place we were too long unwilling to go. We want to go back and kick it away. We want to remove that stone and tell it that it has no place there. That is our special place; ours and God's.

A little whisper stops us from going back. That still, small voice tells us to leave it, to let it stay.

"Upon this rock," the Voice says. "Upon this rock."

"'…upon this rock I will build my church, and all the powers of hell will not conquer it." - Matthew 16:18b

11 | I Spy

"Come and see what our God has done, what awesome miracles he does for his people!...Come, let us rejoice in who he is." -Psalm 66:5, 6b

Do you see what I see?

For generations, God's people rejoiced together in His good works. He worked among His people in such a visible way that everyone saw, and everyone knew, that these miracles were the work of His hand. Israel rejoiced in the broad strokes of His divine paintbrush, watching His plan unfold before their very eyes.

That is not so much the case today. We are living in a highly individualized, privately personal, "specific society." That is to say, we are not so interested in His broad brushstrokes any more; we are drawn by the nitty-gritty, the fine details that answer our smallest prayers.

And when we find those tiniest accents in His work, we are anxious to share them with the world. We pray that everyone can see the God we see, to know Him as we know Him, to find Him working in their lives as we plainly see that He is in ours. We can't believe that anyone could fail to see this, could fail to rejoice in this with us, or could fail to understand God's divine artistry in what we are seeing.

At the same time, we are not fully interested in giving away our entire secret, our whole gift. It makes us feel special to know that God would do this for us. What an honor to know how He works in our lives and how this gift is a piece of His special favor for us. We want others to see, but we do not want to show it all to the world. We want to savor some for ourselves and pray for others to get the hint without stealing our glory.

It is part of our intimately private relationship with God.

We need to feel that chosenness. It seems to make God more tangible if we can see what He has done or is doing or promises to do in the most minute area of our lives, if we can put some kind of label on His activity here. It speaks about our life and our blessedness.

Our blessedness, we would like to share with the world. We want to show them that we have encountered the true and living God and share with them His marvelous glory by describing, without fully disclosing, what He is doing. We describe the place He is meeting us, the far corner of the playground. We describe the very specific way He has answered our greatest need of the moment or our most pressing question. We want others to see.

This, we think, will give them a glimpse of God's glory (as manifested in His greatest accomplishment – us). It will instill in them a longing to find something as beautiful without sacrificing our own gift.

This is why we keep our eyes moving, never focusing on His beautiful blessing even as we savor its presence. This is why we never soak it in or let it captivate us publicly; only privately, where we can be sure that no one is following our gaze. No one sees exactly as we see, which keeps this perfectly special between Lord and child. We win. Because we see it and you didn't catch it right away.

But it is not good to keep such secrets. It is not good to hold the Lord close and not follow His greatest command to spread His message. So we come up with vaguely specific descriptions of His work here and spout to believers and non-believers alike:

I spy with my little eye... some completely specific, tiny little thing that God has done in my life in response to a particular situation that doesn't really affect anybody but me.

It could be that God sent a Good Samaritan to change our flat tire on the side of the road. Or that He gave us a breakthrough on a big budgeting problem at work. Or that He found a way for our distant relatives to use their frequent flyer miles to visit on a special weekend that we grieved they would miss.

These little things are wonderful, and in many of our lives, this is what we see God doing everyday. But for those who do not know God, and often for those who do, it is difficult to deduce much of God's nature at all from such specific examples.

The unchurched and those who do not know God develop an impression of Him by the way we share His work in our lives. When we try to help them see these little examples, even if we can convince their eyes to find this in the details, they can only shrug and wonder, "So what?" They are not interested in a God of specificity; it is too difficult to predict and more, to understand, a God like that. This is what raises the troubling questions that we often face in our evangelism – the question of why God does something here and not there, in this situation but not that one. Most of us have no answer and shuffle our feet as we scurry away to let the question run in our own minds and terrorize our faith.

This is also the burning question of those who believe in God and who have seen Him work wonders but do not find the answers they desperately seek. Why is God doing that in your life and not mine? they ask when we try to get them to see in the details. Our responses here are worse and usually less than uplifting, as we try to concoct some reason why we are holier or more favored or better discipled than our brother or sister whose heart is questioning.

There is nothing wrong with looking into the details. We should always worship the acts of God in our lives, no matter how big or how small. But like a picture painted in pointillism, it is difficult to show God to the world when we are taunting them with one small dot.

If we gave enough detail, or if we spoke in the broadest terms, they would easily figure it out and we would lose the game. That's the game we are locked in: trying to see something that no one else sees, then trying to convince them that it's blatantly obvious without making it clear what anybody is talking about. Holding close that we have a wonderful secret, teasing them just enough to set them seeking without enough parameters to narrow it down.

Ancient people understood the trap, and they found a way to worship God through the broad and the minute. The Israelites, who worshipped acts of God together, would not communally celebrate the intimate moments, though they certainly understood them.

When they gathered together to remember and celebrate God's work among them, they read from the scrolls of their history. Nowhere in those records does it say, "And remember, you, when God healed Jehozab of his leprosy." Nor does it say, "Celebrate and rejoice, remembering what the Lord did for Desileia when her toddler wandered away but returned home safely."

No. These are, indeed, some of the miracles of God, but they are very personal. They were probably great signs to those individuals of God's presence and mercy in their lives, but they were not a message to the greater tribe. It would be hard to rally around such private memories, let alone design a memorial feast or festival to perpetuate the reading and remembrance of them each year (though it may have been all Jehozab and Desileia could talk about).

And where do you draw the line? Which events like these get recorded and which do not? If any peoples were to write the entire history of God in their community, in the smallest detail and each point of the painting, there would be neither enough paper nor ink in the world.

Our God is real and tangible; He is constant. His attributes are the same from the beginning of time until the end of it. That is what is most lost in our attempts to get the world to see Him as we do. We do not tell them of God's nature; instead, we tell them of His intervention. It is our attempt to show them how He intercedes in this world and loves everyone, but it raises more questions than answers. It turns Him into a personal deity, a concept of our individual imaginations, and something ever-changing.

This is where we would be wise to take a lesson from the ancient peoples. They gathered together to read and remember His work, and it was truly His work, the art of His very nature.

They remembered when He appeared as a cloud before them, and fire at night, to guide their way through the wilderness. That is not personal; it is a broad brushstroke of His guidance.

They remembered when He scattered nations before them as He led their armies into victory in the Promised Land. That is not private; it is the broad stroke of His provision.

They remembered when He fed and clothed them in captivity and strengthened their faith in tribulation. That is not specific; it broadly displays His sustenance.

They read and remembered the words of the prophets – men like Isaiah and Jeremiah – who foretold the coming of the Messiah and the redemption of the world. That is not secret; it is a broad brushstroke of His promise.

Everyone saw, and everyone remembered.

This is the image we need to be sharing with the people we engage today. When we set out to help them see what we see, the beauty and glory and grace that drew us to our God, we need to use the grandest, most visual display possible. We need to draw their eyes to the boldest elements of God. We need them to see not His specific intervention but the very nature of His fullness.

We need to start showing them the things that build community, the things that point to our constant God.

I spy with my little eye... the peace that eliminates all worry.

I spy with my little eye... perfect love.

I spy with my little eye... the joy that passes all understanding.

I spy with my little eye... the goodness that lets me hit the ground hard and bounce instead of break.

I spy with my little eye... a Man on a tree in the open field of Golgotha.

When we start working in this way, we invite those around us to begin to see as we see and to know God as we know Him. We invite them to know Him as He truly is, the God we have seen in the Bible, and to begin developing their own personal, private, wonderful memories with Him. We invite them to become a new dot in the picture He is painting.

And we know we do not lose because someone else sees as we see. We never lose by revealing the richness of God.

The beauty of God's artistry is magnificent in any eye, and how much more so when all who stand before it are invited to see fully. When no eyes remain focused on the details, the fine dots of its composition, the painting takes on new meaning and builds the community of God – a community content to stand and stare and marvel at His masterwork together, knowing and praising His work by its broadest strokes but cherishing that little place that each member holds in the finest detail.

"For the features of the earth take shape as the light approaches, and the dawn is robed in red." - Job 38:14

12 | Jump Rope

"When people fall down, don't they get up again? When they start down the wrong road and discover their mistake, don't they turn back? Then why do these people keep going along their self-destructive path...?"
- Jeremiah 8:4b-5

Sometimes, life skips along. Everything seems to be going our way, and we have tapped into that great promise and assurance of God. Every day harnesses the beauty of His majesty, the goodness of His grace.

Sure, there are still times when something comes along that tries to trip us up, to cause us to stumble, but we see most of those things coming and hop right over them, soaring above the threat with flying colors.

Our whole bodies are engaged in the process – our arms swing back and forth, round and round, while our legs power us through and lift us over our troubles. Our breath is regulated in rhythm with our movements, and we feel our strength building. Each skip of a step ends with our feet firmly planted back on the ground, and this only boosts our confidence.

That confidence leads to risk as we find new ways to move effortlessly through the blessed life God has gifted us. Maybe we try for awhile on one foot or with a bit of a double hop, just to feel that solid feeling of hitting the ground again and again. How good it feels beneath our feet! How stable and reassuring!

Every muscle group burns with the activity, that incredible tingling feeling that lets us know something is happening inside us on a level we could only imagine and hardly understand. On the most minute level, we are entrenched in the moment and nearly vibrating from its awesome power.

We jump again and again; our hearts race. We have complete control, trusting in our feet to guide us and our bodies to respond accordingly. Until the next little hang-up circles around and...

Trips us up.

The smallest snag in our feet or in our circumstance sends us sprawling, half-forward but fighting to stand upright. We battle the urge to fall, knowing that as firmly as the ground received our feet, its harsh surface will cut our hands like glass. We let go of anything that is not an asset to our balance and wobble like a windsock until we finally steady ourselves, shaken but still upright.

Then, inexplicably, we bend over and pick everything back up to put that rhythm and that little skip back in our step exactly as we had left it before it tripped us up. This time, we will be more vigilant and more focused on our tasks. This time, we will have more control over our lives and watch our feet carefully to ensure they are in perfect sync with our hands and our bodies.

This time, our confidence builds more quickly. We remember this rhythm and the way it feels to have God's goodness on our side, the way we put each foot down firmly in His grace. The tingling surges through us sooner than we expected, but only because we are comfortable here. We are comfortable knowing that we are back in control and everything is as it should be.

But the longer we stand in one place with our arms swirling around us and our feet coming down on the same little patch of solid ground, the more monotonous it all seems. This life, while still exhilarating in its predictability and confidence, is much too plain and too boring. We hope and we pray, even while we thank God for the gift of this place, that He is calling us to something more, to something wild and crazy and daredevilish.

We trust that this is exactly His call, and in the blessedness, we start to test our own abilities or perhaps we are testing God.

We want to see if we are able to take this grace with us wherever we go or maybe if God is able to follow where we are headed and the challenges that exist in our world. We want to start showing off a little bit, demonstrating loudly and almost foolishly how strong and steadfast we are in this place and how God is with us no matter when, no matter where, and no matter what.

We start with a little double hop, just the simple exercise of putting our feet down more than once and understanding they will still stick. It speeds up our rhythm just a little, but it makes us feel like things are moving along, like we are progressing somehow.

Then a skip step here or a cross-legged hop. Then, we start bringing obstacles in front of us so that we do not simply have to watch our step but watch life come at us from all sides, complicating our steps but not taking the ground out from beneath our feet.

While we show off, test the limits of our assurance and of God's blessing and attempt to pull Him into our performance, we lose a little grip on our control. As we get a little lax, circumstance that we thought we had a handle on comes around to trip us up again.

And we stumble, falling forward and letting go of everything in a desperate attempt to keep our balance. All that we once thought was in our hands hits the ground with a smack and our hands are soon to follow, scraping against the harsh surface with a sharp sting that is decidedly less spectacular than the warm tingle of our hearts racing and our breath pounding and our lives being in perfect rhythm.

As we bend down once more to take a new grip on life, we wonder if we truly want to pick it all back up. We want that euphoria, that existence in God's presence that is indescribable, but the task of handling everything ourselves is overwhelming. We understand that it was by our own hand and our own unsettledness that we fell so hard to begin with. We held our circumstance in our hands; we brought it around as an obstacle to our feet. We failed at this one thing – at putting our feet down – because we could not do everything.

So there is the choice: that awesome feeling of having everything together and knowing we can only experience God's blessing if we commit to the boring, monotonous idea of standing in one place forever, having our hand on everything and controlling our circumstances, letting our feet hit the same piece of ground over and over and over again until our eyes are so tired of the scenery that we simply close them and feel like we are missing out on something but knowing that something is not here.

Or we can drop control of our circumstance, free ourselves for a challenge and for the glory of God.

It is a choice that God already made for us. His divine plan does not call for us to control everything, to put our circumstances before us again and again only to find that happy little step that puts us over the top and back on solid ground. He has created a way for us to engage our whole bodies without controlling our whole world, to still experience that tingle that lets us know He is there without tripping ourselves up by putting anything in our own way.

He asks us to go Double Dutch. He tells us that this experience of His goodness is not dependent on our circumstances and that if we try to control everything, we will most certainly end up stagnant. And bored. And wondering why it seems this life is passing us by while we are desperately clinging to that once-upon-a-time feeling that still sends chills up our spine but misses something nonetheless.

He tells us that He will hold the ropes, that He will control the circumstances so that we can focus on just one thing, the one thing that He has called each of us to – living the faithful life.

The faithful life is finding solid ground no matter the circumstances. It is understanding that there are many things that are out of our control, and many others that should be out of our control if we want to move at all.

The faithful life is being able to pull a stunt every now and then and not risk dropping everything and falling flat on our face. Our hands are free to help us keep our balance, no matter what we are trying to do. We could turn ourselves upside down and plant our hands on solid ground if we wanted to, skipping through life in a handstand. Or we could hold our arms straight out and use them to steady ourselves on ground that is less than solid, if we land sideways or backward or on a ball. (Or off the ball, as some of us seem to live.)

The faithful life is what opens us up to both follow God and take Him with us, because we know that He always has one hand on our circumstances. Maybe the world controls a part of it, and maybe there are still times we start to trip, but we can truly engage our whole selves – our feet, our hands, our eyes, our hearts – to respond.

We can turn around in circles and see on one end how the world tries to manipulate our circumstance, how it is swinging and swirling these situations in front of us and daring us to overcome them. The world flinches a little, trying to fake us out and show us that we have no power here. The world is in control, and it wants us to know that at its whim, our situation can become unpredictable and treacherous.

The world wants to tell us that when it chooses, we will have to slow down. Or speed up. Or take a higher road. The world wants to tell us that we are its victim, caught in its clutches by a rope just long enough to hang ourselves.

Then, we turn another half-circle and find the other message. We look up and see God standing there. He has been there the whole time, holding on to something that could have been our downfall. His power, His hand have redeemed our situation while we used the fullness of our faith, our strength, our steadfastness, and His mercy to set our feet down.

Each time we stick the landing, our faith and confidence grows. There is a softness, a stillness, and a brief moment of rest, but there is one aspect of this exercise more rewarding, more exhilarating, more wonderful.

It is that sound that comes when our circumstance hits the ground. When life runs up against that firm foundation with an addicting *snap* that sends it flying in the other direction, unable to penetrate terra firma.

It is a sound that sickens the world, frustrating its wisdom and manipulation. But to us, that is a beautiful sound, so beautiful that we use it as the beat to our song, the music of the playground, and the rhythm that guides our movement.

That is the foundation and the call of our worship - that striking sound of life meeting God.

"Happy are those who hear the joyful call to worship, for they will walk in the light of your presence, Lord.... You are their glorious strength." - Psalm 89:15,17a

13 | Merry-Go-Round

"So I tell you, don't worry about everyday life–whether you have enough.... Doesn't life consist of more...?"
- Matthew 6:25

But we are so excellent at worrying! Some might even say that worry is what we do best.

We worry about the big things. We worry about the little things. We worry about things that have no bearing on us, things we can do nothing about, and things we wouldn't do anything about even if we could.

We latch on to a worry, tighten our grip around its rails, and then run it in circles in our minds. Round and round and round we go, running these unnecessary thoughts through our mind until they gather enough speed and enough force and enough energy behind them that we start to wonder whether we're still running them around or they are dragging us with them.

The colors of our lives start to blur before us, all formed from our worry. The red of anger, the pink of shame. The yellow of fear, the blue of grief. The oranges and purples. It makes us all a little green.

And just when we can run these thoughts around no more, as we measure our own strength and speed against the developing momentum of the worry itself, do we dare let go? Of course not!

We jump right onto the worry-go-round and let it take us for a ride.

As our feet land on worry, we know we are not ready for the centrifugal force that would throw us right back off were we not holding on so tightly. We struggle to gain our bearings; we tighten our grip on our worries and fade into the blur.

It doesn't have to be worry; just about anything can give us that dizzying sensation.

It can be a secret sin that rules our lives, one we thought we conquered long ago that somehow continues to rear its ugly head.

It can be hate, the kind of hate that makes us fume when we think of anything near that situation.

It can be disappointment, especially when we watch someone else bask in the glory of something we worked so hard for or yearned so painfully to earn.

It can be grief, noticing after years or even decades that something lost can never be regained or someone lost is missing that once-in-a-lifetime event.

It can be any number of pains or sadnesses or wounds from our past, the ones we thought we healed or at least repressed enough to allow us to function.

The common theme is not the worry or the sin or the disappointment. The common theme is the way these things work themselves into our lives, the way they always seem to circle back around. When they find us again, and they always do, we have to find a way to deal with them.

We can, as we do when we initiate our worries, grab hold and start running them around in our minds. But what if... this? Or what if... that? Then, what if...? But only if.... And then, there's always.... In an infinite universe, the possibilities are endless for any situation, and this is a rut we should not get ourselves into (despite how tempting and relatively easy it is to do).

We can try to ignore them, but unless we're vigilantly aware and engaged, the force of the motion with which our greatest pains come back to us will sweep us away. Like a whirlpool, they will drag us in smaller and smaller circles until we are sucked down into the deepest vortex. We resurface somewhere far removed from the whirling, but who knows when or where.

We can grab hold and run in the opposite direction, using our legs to power the wheel backward and slow, if not stop, it altogether. But we can no more easily succeed at this than we can turn back time; it is not within our power to take our worries, our disappointments, or our regrets back.

We can jump right into the middle of the wheel and take a short ride, demonstrating our dominance and balance before jumping back off on the other side and avoiding disaster altogether. This is what the cool kids try to do, but we all know the mockery of coolness: the cooler we try to be or the cooler we think we are, the more likely we are just being foolish and are about to be thrown off the ride and into the gravel. Face-first. With the whole playground watching.

We can reach out one measly arm and attempt to stop the wheel with a simple block. But our arm is neither strong nor steady enough. More likely, the impact will knock us off our feet and in our effort to save ourselves, we'll grab desperately for something to hold onto and realize too late our handle is our worry. It will drag us around, our feet leaving dusty trail marks around the circumference of the go-round, a lasting testimony to our futile resistance.

Certainly, we do not want to put ourselves in a position where we are out of control, where the forces of physics and these obsessive entities dictate our response.

There is one other instinctual reaction. We could take a step back, safely away from the whipping vortex and for a moment, just watch, watch the blending and the swirling of the colors, watch the blur that could easily be our lives. This, too, is dangerous. The colors can so mesmerize us that we zone out and live a zombie-like existence, aloof of the world, no longer participating in anything.

We should not simply remove ourselves from the situation. That is denial, and it guarantees that each of those colors will only circle back to catch us again, forcing our hand in the same decision.

Then, what is Godly? How would the irony of the wisdom of our God choose to respond? There must be a way because it was He, the Creator, who set the world spinning in circles from the beginning of time. Surely, He devised a way to respond wisely, humbly, and in a seeker's spirit to those things that only come back around and back around and back around in our lives.

He has.

He begins by reminding us that this is His creation, this cyclical nature. Just as the world spins on its axis, so, too, we can expect our lives to come full-circle from time to time. Look at the way it works, He reminds us. This motion allows the sun to heat and cool the earth daily, yearly, in a life-giving circuit that makes nearly the whole of the planet inhabitable.

He reminds us to never take things too quickly. There's no need to rush, no hurry. Were the world to spin any faster, it might dislodge from its axis and hurtle toward the sun, burning creation alive.

He admonishes us to let things settle, to let them seek their rest. Though this ride – this worry, fear, disappointment, pain, grief, or whatever – seems demanding now, time will steal its thunder and we can look again when things start to slow down, when the pace seems more reasonable. If we fling ourselves on when life is moving top speed, it will only fling us right back off. He understands that.

He tells us to take control. To not stand idly by and watch our troubles spin out of control, for there is no telling when they might stop on their own or who might come to perpetuate their motion. Or worse, who else might get caught up in our mess. But before we act impulsively and reach out to slow the wheel, he reminds us of what we already know: that will never work.

Instead, He prods us to plant our feet, to stand firmly on the solid ground of His work. His strength. His mercy. His peace. Look carefully, He continues, and find the right handle – the one most solidly welded into the situation, the one least likely to fly off, the one most firm to grasp. As it approaches, He leads us to lean slightly forward, put the right force in our bodies and then, reach out and grab hold.

Our feet stay planted. Our body straightens as we use our strength and the power of physics to pull back on the wheel and stop the worry. Just like that, it stops because of the strength of wisdom and obedience.

We're left standing, holding the idle-go-round and wondering what's next.

"Let go."

When we let go, a soft wind blows and sets the wheel in motion again, a gentler motion. There's a slight creak as the wheel turns on its rusty axle, a piece of the playground weathered by many years exposed to the elements. And then we see it....

The blur that made us dizzy, that mesmerized our eyes, is more beautiful in simple colors. Divided out, apportioned perfectly, they make the wheel a spinning art and a piece of glory. Turning slowly, it is much clearer and very beautiful. Somehow, turning slowly, it is even more glorious than standing still.

It is our lives that feel like the blur, like everything is moving too fast and there's too much to deal with. When we slow it down and stop trying to make everything move faster, stop obsessing over our worries and our fears and our disappointments and our pains, stop trying to find a way to hold on until we pass out or throw up or both, we see the colors start to separate.

That's how God sees it. He sees the millions of colors that paint our lives as perfectly apportioned pieces of a beautiful whole, and He appreciates them all the more when they are moving gently. A Godly, humble pace that neither denies nor defies the cyclical motion He ordained in the universe.

A pace that shows we are not victims of our worry but that even our worry adds to the beautiful tapestry and vibrant rainbow that is our lives. The red of anger... or of fiery passion. The yellow of fear... or of light. The blue of depression... or breathlessness. The pink of shame... or of tenderness. The green of envy... or of newness and growth.

No matter what they define for us in any particular cycle, these colors circle around and around and around again and again and again and, at a decent pace, create not a blur but a stunning display.

This is the display that drew us to the playground in the first place. It is the one that inspired us that these colors would look beautiful in motion, which we took to an unnecessary extreme as we always do. Now that we're content to journey as gently as the wind blows, we are ready to hop on and take this ride as many times as it will come around.

Coming full-circle makes us whole.

Through the eyes of God, we find the merry in this little go-round.

"And we know that God causes everything to work together for the good of those who love God and are called according to his purpose for them." - Romans 8:28

14 | Miss Mary Mack

"...what's the use of saying you have faith if you don't prove it by your actions?" – James 2:14

Voices carry, and words command attention. From the furthest corners of the playground, the rhythm of a simple rhyme draws crowds. People drop whatever they are doing and wander over, turning an ear to hear the lyrics and committing them to memory so that one day, they too might play this game and draw the interest of an entire world.

The words are simple enough, repetitive even. Miss Mary Mack Mack Mack all dressed in black black black. They are words we practice in secret until we know them well enough to put on a performance, until we have committed them to our tongues and are assured we will not slip and embarrass ourselves.

It is a good place to start, but these games are not poetry readings; they are not recitation of rhymes. That would get old fairly quickly, for what else do we know about this Mary Mack? We only know her surface, that she dresses in black adorned with silver buttons (all down her back back back). Were there only these words, the audience would disperse as soon as they gathered. Who cares how Mary Mack dresses?

Yet this is how we approach the words of our faith. We practice them in secret, committing to memory the words we will use to let people know we are faithful without sounding hokey or brainwashed or oblivious to the challenges of the real world. We want to create with our words an attractive rhythm, something that will draw the crowds and beg them to hear, but we know our words only demand a certain level of interest.

The crowds will listen for a few moments. They will try to learn the rhyme themselves, to recite this poem in their own tongue. Therefore, it can be nothing too difficult or controversial or contrived. It must flow naturally from our lips and theirs, and it must stick firmly in their minds so that once they leave our presence, the words echo in their heads.

"Jesus loves me; this I know, for the Bible tells me so."

"God is good; all the time. And all the time; God is good."

The rhymes are catching, but they are shallow. They are generic words that leave the world wondering.

They wonder what, if anything, of substance we reveal about God with these words. That He loves us because He says He loves us? That He is always good?

That paints a picture of a dictatorial, impersonal God who prides Himself on ego by telling us what to believe and expecting us to chant His mantra. It is not the God we interact with on a daily basis, the One who hears our prayers and responds to our cries and intercedes on our behalf.

We are missing half of the game; we are missing half of the rhythm. There are gestures, hand motions, that tie the rhyme to a series of clapping, slapping, and hand-crossing, creating not just an auditory but an impressive visual display. These motions, too, we practice in secret, perfecting them against a mirror to build confidence in our hands.

We believe in good works as evidence of our faith, so much that we neglect the words. In our hearts, we praise Christ as the inspiration for our good deeds, but our lips remain silent as we focus on getting our hands right. On performing the perfect hand jive that puts our hands above, below, and all around the world's needs and provides strength, support, and solution. We commit to teaching the world the motions, on teaching the principles of service and the specific acts that God calls us to – feeding the hungry, clothing the naked, providing shelter for the homeless or refuge for the stranger. It does not matter what prompts someone to do good, we convince ourselves, as long as good is being done.

But that does not introduce anyone to Jesus. It does not tell them of the personal God who inspires our actions, who encourages us to act upon His promise through our faith. And without the regulating rhythm of the rhyme, it looks more like our hands are seizing than following the pattern, trembling and shaking instead of moving with deliberate motion.

Our practice makes perfect and bolsters our confidence. The more confident we are of our tongue and our hands, the more willing we are to risk drawing the attention. We know the rhyme, and we know the rhythm. We begin teaching others the same way we taught ourselves – one piece at a time.

We teach them first the rhyme, the feel-good sayings that oversimplify our God and we hope to round out any misconceptions with the rhythm.

The key is both together, the rhythm and the rhyme, working in harmony.

We join forces with someone just starting, someone learning the moves on their own, and stand face-to-face with them to complete the presentation. Two voices more powerful than one, our words spread across the playground, underscored by the sound of clapping and slapping. Onlookers gather, and our hands crisscross in perfect synchronization with our playmate, completing the rhythm that calls to the world.

We are not afraid of messing up, of losing the beat or slowing down. Instead, as we continue, we grow more confident. The way our hands guide our words and our words guide our hands, it would be foolish now to mess up. It would be nearly impossible to falter.

We look at the faces of those watching, some moving their lips to learn the rhyme; others moving their hands to learn the rhythm. Everyone just stands there, mesmerized by the display and longing to join in. They break off into pairs and begin teaching each other, trying to copy the rhythms and trying to remember the rhymes.

Now is our time to shine, our time to take control and show that it is not as difficult as it looks. Without any warning to our partner, without even a wink of the eye, we start to speed up. Slowly at first, until we are sure he is following with us, and then faster and faster until we lose all control. Our tongue ties itself in knots, refusing to speak any words, and our hands wrap around each other until they simply quit and fall to our sides.

It is our fatal flaw: paying more attention to the watching world than the inherent wisdom in our hands and tongue, we have outpaced ourselves. Either our hands move faster than our words can keep up or the other way around, we speak faster than we can act. Both result in the destruction of everything we were trying to do here. Both get us out of rhythm, out of sync not only with our partner but with ourselves.

The only way to get back into the groove, to catch up with ourselves, is to start over. We have to go back to the beginning and slowly let our words and our deeds come back into harmony with one another, neither leading and neither following. They must come back together in perfect unison and create again the stirring rhythm. Then, we must learn to pay attention and listen, perform every motion diligently and with great discipline. These are not robotic movements; they are not something our hands will do without our conscious thought. Nor are they mindless words. These are the words that characterize and inspire our motion.

We aspire to greater quickness, that often elusive ability to turn immediately to faith and put our hearts into action. We should aspire to that – to making God our first thought instead of our last, to learning to respond by faith in word and in deed instantly and unwaveringly, trusting in the innate understanding that has enveloped our hearts.

But neither our words nor our hands will ever be perfect. And it was never our perfection that made anyone stop and stare. In fact, our imperfection eased the tension and let everyone share in a good-hearted giggle before daring to try themselves. It was the rhythm, the voices in tempo with the intricate beat underneath, that drew people in.

It is the fullness of the rhythm that keeps them coming back.

The rhythm falls back in motion, and all over the playground, voices can be heard singing the rhymes. Claps and slaps and eruptions of giggles pop up from every direction as people of all ages, those just learning and those who know this rhyme by heart, fall in and out of beat with each other or push beyond the limits of their coordination.

Two by two, the grounds fill with pairs and partners copying the rhythms of the Lord, combining the sometimes oversimplified but often catchy words of faith with the complex work of the hands.

Giggles fade to a solid rhythm as people mature and come to understand the delicate relationship forming between their words and their actions. The longer each player continues in sync, the more natural it seems, and our words become tied to our hands.

Each individual chorus slowly but surely fades into the masses until both the rhythms and the rhymes are in perfect unison all across the open field. One pair joins another in a four-way exercise, then six-way, then eight-way until all of the hands join together in a glorious display of choreographed movement.

Here, the visual aspect takes on new meaning as the motions seem to wrap around this place. It can be mesmerizing, drawing in a new audience even as the circle continues to grow. Nobody rushes. Nobody tries to get ahead. Nobody is falling short and erupting in giggles. Everyone has settled into the cadence of the wisdom of faith.

The rhythm is so perfect that anyone who loses coordination by momentary distraction easily finds his or her way back into the music. The whole world sings by faith, words that may have once seemed trite that never painted the whole picture of God.

But with the resounding thunder of the work of the hands bringing together the message and the mission, this is the most beautiful way to invite others to join the chorus.

The chorus is one of a faith that is not hollow or passive, depending on an impersonal God to save us by His whim. Nor is it a faith of grace by works, which depends entirely on our own efforts. It is the beat of a faith of knowledge combined with a faith of works that fills in the fullness of God.

And when the whole world sings, no matter how trite or narrow or imperfect the words may be, it is a performance that inspires. It instills in others a yearning to learn the words, to learn the motions, to learn the dance.

It is our place to teach them, to keep the rhymes and the rhythms flowing from generation to generation as the echoes continue to spread. We teach them just as we were taught, teaching them first the words of our faith, as simple as they are.

Jesus loves me, this I know for the Bible tells me so....

Then watch, as their hands instinctively start moving to join the choir as the pulse of His people shakes the world.

"So commit yourselves completely to these words of mine. Tie them to your hands as a reminder.... Teach them to your children." - Deuteronomy 11:18-19a

15 | Monkey Bars

"...receiving God's promise is not up to us. We can't get it by choosing it or working hard for it." - Romans 9:16

There was always a line for the monkey bars. My school had one set. The park down the street had one set. Kids wasted their whole afternoon waiting for the chance to climb three little steps, grab onto the first or maybe the second bar, dangle for a few moments, then fall helplessly to the ground.

Day after day, they stood there waiting. Few had the strength to make their bodies move. More than once, a fight broke out as one kid or another tried to push his way to the front of the line or take a second turn after falling off too quickly.

"No," he'd protest. "That was a practice. It doesn't count."

A practice. Monkey bars are one activity where practice never helps. Either you have the upper body strength to make it or you don't; it's not like after grabbing that first bar for the twentieth, thirtieth, fiftieth time, some light bulb will go off in your head, and you'll "get it."

No. Monkey bars are a go or a no. Do or die. And on my playground, where the pit beneath the monkey bars was cushioned with a few inches of gravel, "die" was a real option. Some kids sat on the sidelines watching, afraid to step up to that bar, to grab hold and look down on the sharp, pointy edges of rock that glistened grey in the sun and awaited their defeated *thud*.

They knew they couldn't do, so why assuredly die?

Still, kids too numerous to count stood in line every day for their turn to practice. You could see just watching them how desperately they wanted to cross that treacherous terrain.

Each day, their preparation took longer and longer, each child stepping up with more caution and care. They would grab hold of the first bar, then spend a good thirty seconds adjusting and readjusting their grip. A slight sway began to build in their bodies, preparing the momentum they believed would carry them across the gulch. Determination stilled behind their eyes.

This time, each thought. This time, I will make it.

"Shut up!" the daredevil would yell to the side as other kids grew short in patience and nearly pushed him off the platform. With a shake of the head and in a desperate attempt to regain his composure, the kid always readjusted his hands on the bar, swayed his body, and launched himself...

...right into the gravel. Before he could even stand, the next adventurer had a strong hold on the first bar, carefully positioning his grip.

And so it went every day. A whole line of practicers right into the pit, scraping their knees and sending a cloud of fine dust into the air. Nobody ever got better.

Nobody ever gave up. There's something to be said for their tenacity. But I wonder how many understood that the monkey bars would never fall victim to all the determination in the world. I wonder how many knew that practice would never make perfect, that they would need to take a different. I wonder if anyone considered strength over will, muscle over intent, training over practice.

I wonder how many of us consider that today.

Our tendencies to overestimate the value of practice can be seen most clearly in our response to our failings, our sin. There is none among us without sin and yet, we are so reluctant to admit our weaknesses and the places we struggle most. We believe we can gain the upper hand by waiting to address them, watching others step up and fail, learning from their mistakes, and willing ourselves to get past it. Whatever it is, we believe all that stands between us and redemption is our own willpower.

Then we have to come up with excuses as to why we fail again and again. Hey, we wouldn't want to look unholy in front of God's other kids, would we? Someone, someday, has to be the first to make it across, and we all believe that's going to be us.

The secret sin presents itself again, and we steel our nerves. We grip firmly the little bit of righteousness we find in our lives, readjusting our hands and our hearts until we believe there's no way we're falling, no way to slip.

We busy our bodies in the rhythm of our life, building the momentum that we believe will propel us forward, allowing us to cross right over this moment of temptation. We will triumph – purifying ourselves before the Lord while saving face by not having to actually admit any shortcoming. As much as it terrifies us that someone else might find out, we feel most shameful when we approach God knowing our sinfulness.

That's why we need the excuses. And that's why we try to conquer our own darkness before we talk to Him. Heaven forbid the God who knows each hair on our heads and knit us perfectly together in our mother's wombs finds out about that thing we do in secret.

You know, when He has His eyes closed.

Day after day, temptation after temptation, we will ourselves to conquer sin and wind up feeling more like failures than when we first began, covered in the wounds of our fall. We know to take the high road, to lift ourselves high above the dirty, dusty, sharp stones that hold us back. We just don't have the strength.

Then we do something like this: we bend down into the gravel and get our hands dusty. I cannot count the number of times I've watched children do precisely this on the playground, hoping that in some way, the dust and residue of the rock, like a gymnast's rosin, will strengthen their grip.

All that does is get the bars dirty. We cannot expect to get a strong start by keeping sin on our hands; we cannot bring filth into holiness.

God knows that; that's why He brought His holiness into our filth. That is why He sacrificed His only Son for our sakes. He never intended us to spend our lives practicing, straining for holiness and condemning ourselves for failure. His people tried that, remember? We call that the Old Testament.

The only things it takes, God tells us, to take the high road over our sin, are courage and strength. We provide the courage; He provides the strength.

He only asks us to make that first climb, to stand on the brink of the high road and agree to jump off. He only asks us to sway our bodies to His rhythm and be willing to move forward.

This requires that we approach holiness with humility, which demands a certain courage in itself.

But it also requires that we let go.

It requires that we let go of that first bar in order to grab the second. And the second to reach for the third.

We don't like the idea of letting go. Isn't letting go the moment we fall? Isn't a less-than-secure grip an opening for our strength to fail us? All of a sudden, those rocks start to look terribly sharp.

Courage leads us to the platform. It leads us to reach for the high road, for holiness. It emboldens us to accept the challenge of do or die. It even convinces us to slide our feet off the edge and just dangle there for a moment.

Until we ponder the rocks. Then, fear paralyzes us.

Whatever happens next, whether we muster the strength to try and move or we hang there forever, we refuse to fall. Don't move, we tell ourselves. Just hold on.

Our legs flail as we struggle to keep a firm grip. Our hands open and close around the bar, trying to pull ourselves back up just a bit. No, we think as our arms start to quiver. Moving is not an option.

This stillness becomes our enemy as our body turns to dead weight and our strength wanes. Were we moving, our bodies would provide momentum. We would seem lighter, the task less burdensome. Hanging here, we are nothing but a sack of bricks and our worst fear is about to come true.

We will fall. We will fail. The effects of our sin will capture us once more, leaving us scraped and bloody, covered in dust.

That is why we must stay faithful to the one thing, just one, that God has called us to: courage. To approach honestly, to face forward, to keep moving while He provides the strength to carry us through.

It's that simple and yet, so often, we miss that.

We miss that because we feel our unholiness. We don't feel worthy to approach the high road, knowing the filth that covers us. We want to be perfect before we seek God. We want to present ourselves as something He can be proud of, something He can reasonably love.

Which is the opposite of what God desires. He knows we can't take the high road by ourselves. He sacrificed His Son so that we wouldn't have to try. He loves us bloody and broken and defeated, so long as we find the courage to press on. And however many times we're willing to climb that platform, He promises to stand with us and lend His strength.

He promises to guide us, to make our hands steady, and to help us conquer whatever stands between us and holiness. He promises to stand there, cheering us on and rooting for us to make it. He promises to encourage us to try again, as many times as necessary, to harness His strength.

There is none who stands at the end of the course cheering and calling our names like God. No one. A whole host of witnesses gathers around. They cheer and wail and bolster our confidences, but it is God who wholeheartedly believes – no, He knows – that we will make it. There's not a shadow of doubt in His mind... even when there's plenty of shadow in ours for the both of us.

He applauds our courage and cheers us on rung by rung, one small movement at a time.

"You're doing great!" He exclaims, watching. "One small step at a time. Just don't look down!"

And that is the key. Anyone who has made it across the monkey bars knows that is the key – never look down. Never look back. Keep your eyes focused on the end, the final platform, the next solid place you can put your feet down. That is the goal. It is the end. Any other vision, any other sight, will only initiate fear and doubt.

Can I really make it, you wonder? I'm so high up! But when you zero in on the prize and watch it inch its way closer with each move, you are astounded at the power in your own body. You feel the muscles tighten and strengthen in your arms, and your confidence grows with every move.

As long as you don't look down, you know you will make it. You are feeling yourself make it. It is a little unbelievable, but you're doing it! With your eyes focused forward, your hands swiftly but firmly moving from bar to bar, you begin to wonder how you ever doubted yourself.

Your feet steady you on the new platform and finally, you dare look back. You crossed that? You made it through? You took the high road? You feel a little silly that it took so much. Still, you know you could never have done that alone.

Beaming with pride, God wraps you in His arms and helps you to the ground, loving you strongly even as you realize that this same strength held you up there in the first place.

"Be strong and courageous. Do not be terrified; do not be discouraged, for the Lord your God will be with you wherever you go." - Joshua 1:9

16 | Red Rover

"Do not take any of the things set apart for destruction, or you yourselves will be completely destroyed...."
– Joshua 6:18a

Each time God sent the Israelites to conquer a people, a town, or a region, He set guidelines for the annihilation. In some cases, only men were to be killed; women, children, and livestock taken as plunder. In other cases, the richest goods were brought back to the temple as sacred objects or the raw materials to be made into sacred objects. Other towns were burned completely with no life or object left unscorched. That is why it was important for Israel to listen to her leaders, the men (and occasional women) who received God's instructions first-hand.

That way, they could keep themselves from sinning while God led them faithfully into Canaan, their long-promised land flowing with milk and honey.

When God was with them, Israel's army was unbeatable. They marched forward, pressing on hand-in-hand with the Lord, wiping out towns and cities, capturing whomever they could, and settling into their new home along the way. Captives blended into the Israelite community, adopting their customs and laws and in some cases, their God, but many converted the not-so-faithful to pagan worship. God knew the remnants of pagan civilizations were capable corruptors, that even their defiled possessions could alter Israel's altar, and that is why He repeatedly warned His armies not to play this game.

Completely destroy everything, He often said, knowing how easily corrupted His children could be. They did not always listen.

Because we want to plunder. We want to enjoy the spoils of victory, even in war, and have something to show for our strength, our courage, our obedience. We are good soldiers; we really are. Should we not award ourselves some medal, some trophy to remember our triumph?

Our every action is driven by our desire to enhance our resume, our audience, our prestige. The world we're trying to impress is more taken by something than nothing. It is easier to build our reputation with plunder than by displaying a burned-out hole in the ground where something used to exist.

We surround ourselves with the strongest allies, teammates who all but guarantee our success. We hold hands with ego and self, with pride and arrogance, with domination and demanding, with confidence and faith. Then, we cry to what we believe is God's team, to the place we hope our next self-made blessing will come from:

"Red Rover, Red Rover. Send my blessing right over!"

When our summoned blessing is unable to find a weakness in our line, we capture it, too, adding it to our long string of partners in this life we're building for ourselves. It is our plunder for having the strongest army, but it can easily become an idol of gold or silver or worse: it can spread its defilement throughout our lives and poison our whole squad.

It's not that our aspirations are evil in and of themselves; we should always pursue passionately and fully our calling in life. The problem is that our army is unfit, our mission not given the green light, our Commanding General stranded on the other side begging us to stop before we destroy everything in unknowing friendly fire.

Our plunder, we take from a defeated good gift of God and it is we who corrupt the plunder.

That is not difficult to understand if we take a moment to look at the supporting members of our side. Each can easily be seen as a simple corruption of something God would like us to have.

Ego is a corruption of the acceptance He wants us to embrace. He yearns for us to know who we are, who He has created us to be, and to use that personality for His glory. We corrupt it by twisting it to play for our glory.

Pride is a corruption of our thankfulness. We understand our giftedness, His blessings poured out in our lives, and begin to think more highly of ourselves than we ought.

Arrogance is an offshoot of our pride as we begin judging ourselves not by God's standard but by our own. It is a standard that takes our pride and our knowledge of His awesome work in our life and tells us that this somehow makes us better than everyone else.

Domination is our corruption of leadership, of His call to be a leader in the world. Instead of walking softly as Micah says God requires of us, we storm the world to take it by force.

Demanding is our corruption of God's command to stand for righteousness and justice. We've distorted that to mean that we should stand for whatever we decide is right. So we stand bravely and firmly and demand the world respond to us – unfortunately too often about the petty things instead of matters of conscience or holiness.

Even our faith and confidence are corrupted in our ploy because God is not the commander of this army; He still stands on the other side of the field, waiting and pleading for us to call to Him.

Our faith and confidence is only in ourselves and this team of corrupt captives we've captained.

The good news is that most of us, those of us willing to recognize that God must play a part in our endeavors if we hope for lasting success, will eventually get around to completing our team, yelling,

"Red Rover, Red Rover. Send Jesus right over!"

By this point, we're pretty sure of ourselves. We know our team is strong and that anyone should be impressed, if not taken, by our prowess. God will fall right into our strategy, get caught in our web, and become a member of our team. He will be terrifically awed at our ability.

Then, His blessing will flow over everything, and we will be unstoppable. With each of our tools and God on our side, nothing can stop us.

Christ comes running, as He promises to do whenever we call His name.

He's ours, we think as He crosses the open field. We tighten our grip on our surrounding supports and look hurriedly both ways down the line, making certain everyone is paying attention and that they are braced for impact. Christ is coming! He will make this all complete.

With seemingly no effort at all, He bursts through our best defenses, the trap we've set to capture Him. Our hopes of adding Him to our plunder fade, then disappear altogether as He paces in front of our line deciding which of our exhaustively-cultivated assets to take captive first.

Will He take our confidence? Our ego? Pride or selfishness? Demanding or domination?

Please, Lord, we think. You could have at least played along, pretended to have difficulty breaking through. You could have let me think, at least for awhile longer, that I was as strong as I thought I was. You could have pretended for a few seconds, couldn't you, Lord?

Whatever you do, don't take my best friend. Don't take the one I've lived with for so long, who knows me so well and whom I know equally as well. Don't take that one.

He chooses carefully, trying to take a key piece of our defense. He crosses the wide, open, ever-expanding space between our team and His, taking as His plunder one of our allies, our strength that we invested so much in developing.

We watch, head hung low, as He seems to set up camp with our friend further away than from where He came in the first place. Our attention turns quickly to our line. Form up, we yell to rally the troops. Close the gap! Hold tight!

Praying for a different outcome, we yell again,

"Red Rover, Red Rover. Send Christ right over!"

He's had His fun and taken us once, but this time, we are ready. Ready to capture His strength and add Him to our team. Then, for good measure, once we've got Him on our side, we'll ask our friend to come back.

He bursts through more easily than the first time and begins again pacing up and down our line, targeting His next choice of plunder.

Before we know it, we're left standing on the battlefield alone. Each of our allies now gone, we dare look up across the expanse and face the opposition – the opposition that used to be our friends. The players who let us down, who fell victim to the power of Christ and became Someone Else's treasure.

We steel ourselves, knowing it is Christ's move, knowing that at any moment, He's going to call to us.

"Red Rover, Red Rover. Send My child right over!"

Our nerves steel. We rock a little, gaining momentum for the sprint. This is it: do or die. Either we break through Christ's lineup or we, too, become His captive. Our legs churn, our breath heavy, though oddly rhythmic. Our eyes scan back and forth, trying to laser in on the weakest point of His team...

There is no weakness there. Each member is as strong as the others, solid under Christ's command.

And our friends, our beloved friends who we trained to serve our army, have been transformed.

He has restored and redeemed our corrupt plunder.

Pride has become humility; arrogance, servitude.

Ego and self have become integrity and contentment.

Domination has become peace. Demanding is now selflessness.

Confidence and faith are restored to their rightful object: the One and Only God.

They have all surrendered to Him, to another leader, and He has taken them quietly and restored them. They look stronger than ever, beaming with new life and complete resolve. He doesn't have to work nearly as hard to keep them in line as we did! They rebelled and labored to follow our command, but they joyously serve their new Master.

Yet we do not feel betrayed. We don't feel, as we did just moments before, that we've lost everything. Or anything.

We actually feel a little left out. We become aware of our position, standing in the middle of the battlefield alone with nothing behind us to back us up and something wonderful ahead of us. Not an enemy, not yet a friend. But we'd like to be friends.

We'd like to be allies. We want that strength, that joy, and that radiant glow for ourselves. We long to not have to fight any more, to not waste time setting our own traps. We ache for Him to restore us, too.

Our legs slow to a walk and our breathing normalizes. Wiping the sweat from our brow and sweeping a stray hair out of our eyes, we step calmly forward and fall into the arms of Christ.

He catches our weary body and holds us tight, then pulls us into His line where we are strengthened anew by our redeemed soldiers. A small smile crosses our face as we look across the now-empty field to where our army once camped. The world is setting up a new base there, building a new force, but we are not concerned.

Even when the world calls us over, we know His strength will flow through us. We will run, though we will not need to run hard, and bust through the world's best defenses. Plunder and captives in tow for His redeeming work to continue, we will return anxiously to Christ, grateful for our Captor and Commanding Officer.

"But thanks be to God, who made us his captives and leads us along in Christ's triumphal procession. Now wherever we go he uses us to tell others about the Lord...." – 2 Corinthians 2:14

17 | Sandbox

"They yelled, threw off their coats, and tossed handfuls of dust into the air." - Acts 22:23

There's something about sand that beckons us to touch it. It sparkles in the sun and beseeches us to take our shoes off, climb in and feel the grains between our toes. Though each grain is coarse, their combined effect is smooth and enticing.

We gratefully accept the sandbox's invitation every time, but its pleasure soon wears off. Once we are in there, loading a shovelful into this bucket or pushing a small rift aside to bury our hands or our feet or our whole bodies, we realize how futile and temporary our efforts are.

These grains, they are slippery; they settle right back down into rest and are not moved for long. They defy our greatest efforts to make anything of them but individual grains, each with a mind of its own.

Our bucket fills and overflows before we dump it all out and start over. Our hands hit the ground underneath while the rough edges of each crystal exfoliate our skin. Under the weight of the dune, the heat of the sun fades; it is always cool and refreshing. Maybe that is part of the draw.

We get lost in the moment, feeling the way it runs through our fingers and falls with that gentle sound that begs us to do it again.

And again and again until what began on top has sifted to the bottom and the bottom has become the top. Again and again until our eyes cross watching one piece of sand fade into the next in a cascading sea.

How often it seems that we have become the world's sand. How often we feel like this world has taken its shoes off and walked all over us, squishing us betweens its toes. How often we fall, less than gracefully, back from where we thought the world had lifted us. How often we find ourselves at the top only to be shuffled and sifted back down to the bottom.

The world loves to do this to its people, to the individual little specks that make up the cosmic shiftiness. We know this because we have lived it.

We know what it is to be taken advantage of, to commit to one thing only to find the fine print too late that tells us we are in for the long haul. That is the world walking all over us.

We know what it is for everything to come crashing down at that lowest moment, when we aren't sure where the money will come from for more groceries and a letter in the mail declares we owe more than we expected to the gas company because of an "accounting error." That is the world squishing us between its toes.

We know what it is to be lifted up, then tossed aside; to be discarded or pushed away; to be rejected, dislocated, and lost in darkness beneath the weight of the world; to blend into the sea of one of a billion.

If it seems that as Christians, we face more of this than those who do not know Christ, that is entirely possible. Something about the way we sparkle in the Son taunts the world to touch us. And the world particularly enjoys accepting that invitation, trying to mold and move us.

But through the grace of God, we know what it is to be moved.

God's grace makes us the sand that prefers to fall through the world's fingers, that refuses to be molded or shaped into anything. His grace makes us able to fall and find our rest once more, to nestle into a little spot between this other grain and that one and know there is still a place for us here.

His grace makes us that frustrating little speck that refuses to stay where you've put it and falls into the dug-out space, fills the hole and starts an avalanche.

The world moves and molds, but nothing ever stays. Its best attempts fail as the pile of sand before it evens out and falls flat. For awhile, the world rests and buries its hands under the little specks, trying to reach that place where it isn't so hot, where there is coolness and refreshment before lifting those fingers again and subverting the cause above them.

That is part of the world's plan – to dig in beneath the movement and let things settle before bursting out and sending little specks flying in all directions.

That is all we have ever been to the world and all we will ever be. We are little specks.

We are little specks that will never amount to anything because we never follow orders. We are little specks that are not worth half the trouble they cause, but that taunt the world into trying anyway.

We are little specks that run through the world's fingers and defy its attempts to manipulate or move us, but in God's hands we are much more than an aggravating little speck. We are not playthings or pieces to be shuffled around for no good reason at all. To Him, we are one building block, one piece of His master construction in this world.

He knows where He wants us and what our role will be, whether we fall somewhere in the middle of the castle or just on the other side of the moat. He knows which other little specks will surround us, how we will geld and mold together to create something bigger than ourselves under His masterful craftsmanship.

And He sets to work building.

There is always the chance, if we are not tuned in to what He is doing or if we are obstinate in our ways, that we can still fall through the cracks, still be that little speck that falls into the empty space and frustrates the Builder. It is not in His plan, but it is a hazard of the sandbox. Some grains just do not behave.

But God stores a secret weapon, the one to which all grains of sand respond. This is not a weapon of force nor will, intent nor demand. This is not just something else that touches the sand and pushes it around; it is something that comes down and engulfs the sand. It makes each fleck almost magnetic, ready to cling to anything near it and start drawing others in.

It is water.

Living water. The power of God that flows through us, covers us, and gives us that sticking power. The

Holy Spirit that lets us hold our place and be content, understanding that even one small grain of sand gone missing causes the whole structure to shift.

Not only does this Living water allow us to hold our place (or sometimes even cement us into it), it gives us the power to draw on others around us and pull them into their place. It lets us reach out within our little community and encourage one another in filling the role God has set for each of us.

We can look to our left and see another little speck wedged into a place where we understand we would never fit. To our right, there is yet another whose gift and presence is a tremendous asset there. When just about all the water is sapped from our spirits, we are re-infused by those around us who are holding theirs well. For whatever God is building to take shape, we need that liquid coursing through the empty spaces that hold us together.

The world watches quietly as the castle takes shape. They wonder why we are so willing to be a part of this assembly when we were so resistant to their work. They wonder how these little insignificant specks are finding it within themselves to hold together, to build anything. And they quickly grow jealous.

They rant and rave, pacing back and forth, before flying into a fury and attacking. They kick and scream and throw their hands around, flinging grains into the air and scattering little clumps of wet, heavy sand here and there and everywhere. Whatever is left, they dig back in and attempt to make something, anything, work.

They run their fingers to the bottom, then spring them to the top. They dump bucketful after bucketful to the left or the right, but nothing ever stays. Everything falls back into the emptiness and fills the space. What is with these little specks? they scream.

They are just little specks!

Maybe we are just little specks. But God created us that way. Because there is something about little specks: little specks never go away.

They refuse to stay where you put them, and they refuse to let you leave them alone. Whether they were once a part of a magnificent artistry or have yet to find their place, little specks stick with you.

You will find them under your fingernails. You will find them in your shoes. They will fall out of your hair and run down the back of your shirt. They will dig deep into the floor mats of your car, the carpet of your home, the knit in your bed sheets. Little specks will not go quietly.

They get in under your skin until you are almost paranoid, looking everywhere and groaning because you know you can never get rid of them.

For days, even weeks, you will find them everywhere you go. When you think you have found that last little speck hiding, you will open the door to find them tamped into the jamb. You will get frustrated and throw your hands in the air, and dust will swirl around you in a cloud.

It is great fun being just a little speck.

That is what God calls us to be in those moments when it feels like the world's hands are stronger, like we are no longer being sculpted by His master craftsmanship but are only being disturbed, disrupted, and tossed about.

He calls us to be the kind of persistent influence where an encounter does not begin and end at the world's discretion, where we are not victims of the world's fancy. He calls us to have the kind of lasting impression that follows non-believers around.

Ours is a quiet presence, a lingering thought in the back of the mind. We do not need to be pestering or loud or offensive to become a catalyst for God's work. Like the sand, it is in our very nature as disciples of Christ to just hang around, to loiter and cling and hide in the bottom of a shoe somewhere, understanding our presence will be felt without a word.

We are moving through the world, carried in the hair and beach towels and fingernails of those who do not understand the persistence of "insignificant" little specks. Little specks that, no matter how low or how little the light, always find a way to catch a ray and reflect it back, sparkling in the Son and begging the world to come and touch.

Knowing, of course, that the Living Water lingers in us and we are as magnetic as ever, the cornerstone of a new construction in this new place.

"Don't copy the behavior and customs of this world, but let God transform you into a new person.... Then you will know what God wants you to do, and you will know how good and pleasing and perfect his will really is."

- Romans 12:2

18 | Sidewalk Chalk

"Don't be concerned about the outward beauty that depends on fancy hairstyles, expensive jewelry, or beautiful clothes." – 1 Peter 3:3

We spend a lot of our time being surface people, the kind of people who look like they have it all together when you see them from a distance. It is fairly simple to pull off; it is easy to pretend for a short time.

This is the concept known as the social appearance.

It is the one where we take our sporty new hair-do and our minivan full of well-behaved children and pull off the impression of the perfect soccer mom...when at home, we are ready to pull our hair out.

It is a husband and wife holding hands where curious eyes might be watching when they know they haven't spoken kind words to each other in months.

It is a man who wears a suit and works hard every day only to go home to a run-down apartment and open another bottle of alcohol.

For a short time, we can pretend to be anything we want to be or anything we need to be or in certain situations, anyone that someone expects us to be.

Our churches are incredible at perpetuating this idea. Sunday mornings, we gather in lobbies and foyers and sanctuaries and ask, "How are you?"

It is not an honest question; it is one that demands a certain answer: "I'm fine. How are you?"

This is the pretty little church life we have created, and I'm not sure if we have brought it in from our other endeavors or taken it out to the other places. It is idealistic, that everyone everywhere could be "fine" at all times. Then, you have those super-churched people, modern-day saints, who are more than fine. They are "blessed by the best" or "wonderfully created" even when their heavy footsteps and sunken faces betray their words.

For all our effort, this beautiful little world backfires on God, on Christ's mission here. We want to keep up these appearances not so much for ourselves, but for others. We want people to watch us and envy our lives. That makes us feel somehow righteous, like maybe we are doing something right. We know that we have something they should want – Christ – and we assume (incorrectly) that the best way to draw them to it is by being perfect.

All the time.... Say it with me...God is perfect. And God is perfect, all the time.

That's not how the saying goes, and that is not the real world that we live in. God does not demonstrate His perfectness through us; He demonstrates His goodness.

Christians are often accused of being "no fun," and this is what non-believers are talking about. Too often, you find Christians opting out of recess, pretending to be above the whimsy of games and running for no reason and other playful joys like laughing and smiling.

We're sitting over on the sidewalk, drawing pretty pictures and decorating the ground with the colors of the rainbow. And we continue to assume that the more beautiful, the prettier, we make the path, the more people will give up their childish energies and come over to see what's going on.

All of our artwork, the way we so beautifully cover up something so bland, so dull, and so terribly unexciting as the path, has the potential to draw crowds. People who never noticed the grey amidst the green of the grass and the brilliant colors of jungle gyms and slides, now cannot help but look.

As beautiful as it is covered with two-dimensional flowers and rainbows and swirling patterns, they might not notice how bland and dull and grey and, yes, even crooked and cracked it is.

And that is our goal, because nobody would ever take a closer look at any path that was less than smooth, less than perfect, less than beautiful.

Sure, there was a time when the sidewalk was new, fresh and smooth and glistening in the sun as the little flecks of rock picked up rays of sunshine.

But that was forever ago, when the playground was new. This sidewalk has been out in the elements, suffering through wind and snow, rain and sleet, cold and heat, sun and darkness and hailstones the size of apples. It is chipped and cracked and even crumbling in places.

And it has been walked all over, picking up the dirt from thousands of little feet who have never given a second thought to the concrete.

It is beaten down and broken up and in increasing disarray as time wears on.

Weeds are popping through. Grass grows where once there was something solid. Dandelions dot the cracks. Leaves and seeds and bugs, alive and dead, lay scattered across the surface.

It is not as inviting as something new. We know that. We know that when we walk in an area where the sidewalk is cracked or busted or uneven, we start to wonder just what kind of neighborhood we've stumbled upon. Literally stumbled, because the sudden two-inch rise in a square of uprooted concrete knocks our feet right out from underneath us.

Who plays in a place like this? Who follows this sidewalk any more? It is safer in the grass!

That is why we decorate, why we clean up our lives and make them perfectly beautiful - to offer the world the God they are seeking, the one who answers every prayer and takes away every pain and heals every heart. The God we want to show them is the smooth, steady God of easy living.

Then the rains start to fall.

Whether it falls in our lives or in the life of a non-believer, rain is the universal cleanser, and it washes away our pretty little picture. All of the chalk in all of its colors first smears, then smudges, then runs off into the soil revealing a cracked, weathered, dirty, and worn sidewalk.

Our best efforts to pretty the path, to make something beautiful out of something rough, are all for naught and the crowds that had once gathered start to disperse as everyone seeks shelter from the storm wherever they can find it.

Our illusion is destroyed. People start to see that our path was never perfect, that we were just painting over the places we didn't want them to see. Decorating the neglected place in an effort to fool them. They resent us for our deception and for our hypocrisy and self-righteousness. This path is rocky and bumpy and falling apart.

Here, the path begins to stand on its own merit again. It is still cracked, still worn. It still crumbles in some places and buckles up in others. It still doesn't hold a candle to the more brilliant colors of the now-glistening jungle gyms. But it is steady and a welcome refuge for shoes sinking in the mud.

He wants us to see this sidewalk for what it is. It never was perfect, but it is good. It has weathered the storm well. It has enough give poured into its form to accept the harsh handouts of the world and stay steady.

This is still the path from one place to another, from the beginning of our journey to the end. From the noise of the playground to the shelter of the building.

This path is still sturdy. While the waters turn solid ground to mud, sucking shoes and feet and people into is mucky trap, the sidewalk retains its grip. It is not slick. It is not sinking. Cracked though it may be, it still supports the weight of the world walking on it.

The playground gathers rain until our hands no longer find a hold on the monkey bars or our pants soak clean through from sitting on the swings. The sidewalk, though it gathers puddles here and there, keeps us dry while guiding us out of the storm.

This is the God the world truly needs; this is the God they have earnestly been seeking. Not the idealistic God of a perfect world, but the stable presence of the Lord in the world people actually inhabit, where people have to walk and live and play. Not the God of the upper tier, but the God just one step away from the mud.

Sure, He had wanted our travels to be smooth, solid, one journey from end to end, but there is no canopy over God's plan; His best design is exposed to suffer under the laws of nature and the tumult of free will.

It is a comfort to realize His patience and steadfastness in withstanding the elements.

It is reassuring to know that this same sidewalk has always been here. The fresh rain highlights the outline of patches placed over the years, places where perhaps it was too bumpy or too rotted, where maybe it had broken apart completely and had to be cemented back together.

Someone has been here, the people slowly realize. Someone has been caring for this path since the very day it was laid down. Whoever it is understands the integrity of a structure like this and its invaluable purpose here. Whoever it is knows that this is part of the charm of this place, this old beaten, weathered path where generations upon generations of feet have tread.

Whoever it is has seen it not only sufficient but right to keep patching over the broken places, fixing the cracks and the bumps as best as is possible given the resources – time, permission, weather, budget.

This sidewalk has character. It has history. Still not the most attractive or the most beautiful, and far from perfect, it is as much a part of this playground as the rusting chains holding the swings or the steps of the slide where the paint has chipped off or the uneven field covered by clumps of mixing grass and weeds.

People will always flock to this broken place in the rains, even when those rains wash away our beautiful decoration and reveal something less than perfect.

The rains remind us it was never our design or our use of color or the way we labored to create something beautiful here that drew people to this place. They will remind us we needn't work so hard to show God's perfection, but that we should instead focus on radiating His goodness.

We will look back at what we feared was a bland, dull, grey obtrusion, and we will wonder how we ever missed its imperfect goodness.

We will look back to the broken path through the rain and point out the patched places. We will point out the rainbows forming in the puddles, beautiful prisms of color that can never wash away. And we will gasp, breathless, as we see the way the little flecks of rock trapped eternally in the cement catch the light and simply sparkle.

"Is it any pleasure to the Almighty if you are righteous? Would it be any gain to him if you were perfect?"

- Job 22:3

19 | Slide

"...and I thought about the destiny of the wicked. Truly, you put them on a slippery path and send them sliding... to destruction." - Psalm 73:17b-18

Media bombards us daily with falls from grace – the executive embezzling money from his own company, the politician caught in infidelity, the celebrity walking in and out the revolving door of rehab, not to mention non-public figures and their exploits. Seemingly everywhere we look, someone is falling hard and ends up rolling in the dirt.

Since we spend most of our time climbing the ladder, it shouldn't surprise us to watch someone fall every now and again. We're chasing the "American dream," striving to die at least one degree better than our parents. A bigger house, a nicer neighborhood, a fancier title. Maybe something so simple as to be the first to graduate from college or to own our own home.

The only way to get there is to keep climbing, to keep taking that next step up. Some want to climb to the heavens, never stop achieving, but for many of us, we're content with one more rung, with having a life just a little better or a little more at ease. We don't need the world, we say; just a little better view.

One rung up is the most powerful place on the playground. That is the power position we're all familiar with, the one that gives the grandest view and the most power behind your voice. From there, we can see the whole yard, a vision that can be used for good or evil, and our voice carries on the wind. Standing there, we command attention.

There are some, perhaps too many, who never aspire to climb at all. They are content on the ground, gaining nothing, passing by quietly without disturbance.

But for most of us, when we finally reach that top, that place we've struggled to reach, we pause for a moment and look around. We enjoy the broadening landscape and take a deep breath.

Here, we feel steady – a railing firmly in our grips, our feet solid on the rung. We dare not look behind us lest we throw ourselves off balance, though a quick glance over our shoulder is not out of the question. We want to look down, to see how far we've come, and then marvel at our accomplishment.

Me? we think. As short and small and puny as I am, I have made it this high?

For that's how the height makes us feel. Instead of magnifying our bravado or adventure, it almost mocks it and leads us to realize how small we are in that moment. If we look too long at where we've come from, the height alone dizzies us. The dizziness induces fear. The fear, panic.

So before that sets in, we turn our heads and look again over the vast landscape. We resteady ourselves on the rung, adjust our hands on the rails, and consider the possibility of falling. The fall, at least the fall forward, does not look so bad. There is a beautiful metal slide, shining in the midday sun, ready to guide us gently to the ground.

When the time comes, and we know it will come, we just have to remember to keep our feet down and go when we're ready. Then, we'll have a soft landing and be able to stand quickly and get going.

The time is coming, we know, because we feel the pressure building behind us. People are lining up, waiting to start their climb. Some impatient folk have already begun and are now just a rung or two lower than we are, pushing and prodding us to "go!"

We labor to hold onto our top spot, not wanting to give up the glory of the peak. We stand there until the pressure and impatience beneath us or our own over-confident foolishness trips us up and shoves us off the side. If we are lucky, it is a semi-gentle slide down and not a sudden fall, but in either case, we are not ready.

We haven't braced for impact. We haven't put our feet in front of us. So we land face-down in the dirt with a hard thump and get up covered in mud.

This makes us angry and more than a little embarrassed, especially if it's not too long before someone else falls behind us and flattens our face in the ground again. We want to get up, but we are unsure how to go about it.

Is it best to stand right up? Dust off the dirt or keep it on? We are blinded by our supposed slight and focus intently on just one thing: getting back to the top.

We start to stand up and grab hold of the bottom of the slide. Not the ladder, one step at a time, but the end of the slide that just threw us off. If it's enough to come down, then it is surely the best way back up. So we climb.

It's not a climb that can be made easily, but less so if you're trying to stand. You've got to hunch yourself over and walk on all fours, slowly but steadily trying to make your way up the slippery slope.

And a slippery one it is. Our shoes mock us with each step, sliding slightly downward with every forward motion. We brace ourselves, hands and feet, against the short sidewalls as we race toward the top.

Speed is our enemy, and we fall again to destruction. Backward this time, right back into the same mud pit we just crawled out of. Still not feet-first. Still not prepared for the landing.

We crawl up angrier, more set on revenge, ready to reconquer. That place, that high place, seems higher than we remembered, but we are determined.

Deliberately, each step careful and braced, we crawl again toward the top. More hunched over, more solid, and as sure-footed as we can make ourselves. The top comes into view, almost into reach, and the hot metal burns through our hands. A few more steps, and we might just be able to grab...

But no. At the last second, our feet slip again and down into the dirt we fall, getting up quickly a third time with more determination than ever to get back to the top.

Before we even begin our journey, we're brushed aside by someone coming down the slide – feet first, ready for landing.

That's how we want to be! We want to be the kind of person just enjoying the ride, playing well.

That is how God created us to be.

For those of us content to take turns and play by the rules, the slide can be a constant source of strength. We climb sure-footedly to the top, take a few moments to glance around and draw in that clean air, then prepare to return to earth.

We step our feet forward under us and plop down on the hot metal, ready to slide back down. We contemplate our landing to make sure it's as clean as possible, and then we let go and head to the ground.

Let someone else climb for awhile.

We know we have gone as high as we can or as high as we care to, but there's little good to do up there. Our work is on the ground, walking and weaving through the world and spreading the message – the message of what it's like, if only for a moment, to have that spectacular view. If we need to refresh our eyes, we can always climb back up. We know where that ladder is.

God has put that ladder there for us, our opportunity to rise higher, to ascend and for a moment, touch the sky and rejuvenate our spirits. To come closer to Him and escape the dirt for a few minutes, to stand where the holy rain falls first and where the breeze cools the heat of the sun.

He's built that ladder so that we don't have to struggle against the slippery slope, so that we don't have to lug ourselves back up the hard way. Each step, each rung of the ladder, is solid. Each is firmly attached to the railing that guides our hands, each railing cemented into the ground.

That ladder isn't going anywhere; we just have to remember to take it easy on ourselves and actually use the thing. Solid, sure steps progressively higher to that summit once more and then, perhaps with a shout of glee or just shouting for no reason at all, we slide gently back down to where our work awaits.

Still feet-first. Still prepared for landing. Still ready to hit the ground running.

And hit the ground running we do, shouting for joy. Screaming at the tops of our lungs how wonderful that ride was, how unforgettable! We want everyone to know that joy, that free feeling of rising to something higher and holding it all inside as strength for the journey, a memory strongly imprinted in not only the mind but especially in the heart.

We want them to understand particularly the glory and beauty of that descent back to this earth, to the call of humble service and God's great commission. Because life is more than trying to stay on top. It is more than climbing higher and higher and higher and establishing a reign as ruler of the playground.

If only they can see our joy at having come back down, at now being free to roam and wander and walk, to talk with our friends and communities on a comparable level instead of shouting down from above. This is where service happens. It is where evangelism happens. It is where mercy and love and faithfulness and repentance and even redemption happen.

This is where God is doing His work.

This is what separates Him from other gods. He does not seek to remove His followers from the world, to elevate them above the problems here. Instead, He sends us right back down with all of the resources of Heaven behind us. He calls us not to rule the playground but to explore it, not to seclude ourselves above the populous but to humble ourselves and walk among them.

We are to show them the ladder and lead them to His promising path. We are to spur them on and encourage them in their climb, standing at the base and shouting words of encouragement. We are to follow them up or let them follow us and introduce them to the splendor of God as experienced in those highest-of-high moments.

And then, most importantly, we are to show them the soft descent, sliding gently back to earth where their work, too, awaits them. God's work. We are to teach them to steady themselves, keep their feet in front of them, and hit the ground running. Standing, with no dirt on their faces and no scrapes on their knees, redeemed and clean and ready to run and play – raised up and returned to Earth just as the Father Himself comes down to walk among us, doing His work, redeeming and restoring and leading us, as each of us needs... right back around to the ladder.

"For we are the temple of the living God. As God said: 'I will live in them and walk among them. I will be their God, and they will be my people.'" – 2 Corinthians 6:16b

"The sun rises and sets and hurries around to rise again. The wind blows south and north, here and there, twisting back and forth, getting nowhere. The rivers run into the sea, but the sea is never full. Then the water returns again to the rivers and flows again to the sea."
- Ecclesiastes 1:5-7

Life is full of the backs-and-forths, the ebbs and flows of disappointment and triumph, defeats and victories, giggles and tears. From a very young age, most of us are trained in handling these situations.

"You don't always get everything you want." The ebb.

"Work hard, and you will succeed." The flow.

"Life isn't fair." The back.

"God helps those who help themselves." The forth.

Over and over, we are hurled in one direction or another, forward and back with the movement of the universe and at the discretion of what we can only call luck or perhaps fate. When something throws us back or turns our progress around, we surge forward by instinct to recoup our losses and build on our momentum.

But we cannot move forever forward; our gut reaction counter to being pulled back can only provide a small burst of energy, not the sustained motion necessary to keep going. That is why life so easily pulls us back again – we cannot harness our energy in a way that allows us to escape the pull of gravity.

Partly, at least, because we never let go.

Something about this life, with its ups and downs or backs and forths, compels us to hold on tight. We grab hold of it because it is all we have that is tangible, all we can show for our troubles here. What are we, we wonder, without our life? We would be nothing were it not for this, and this... this is the common bond that holds humanity together.

Within us all, we have this life. And whether we like it or not, this life is dictated by forces beyond our control. By gravity, by the pull of the moon, by the swing of momentum that pulls us forward, then back, then forward again only to be drawn back.

So we hold on and learn to take the bad with the good, to use disappointment to fuel our desire for achievement or redemption or reconciliation. Then, we use our victories to strengthen our patience and perseverance for the trials, knowing that in due time, we will swing forth once more and find joy, peace, and goodness.

The inherent limits of momentum steady our hearts. We know we cannot go forward any more than we have gone back, nor can we move back any further than we have moved forward.

But this also means that from our highest highs, we fall to our lowest lows. From the exhilaration of success to the disaster of defeat. From a bright outlook and endless hope to darkness and despair. Somewhere in all of that, the enemy whispers that the joy must have been a pipe dream or a hallucination, at best our imagination run wild. Things are never that good, and shouldn't we know that by now? We were only fooling ourselves.

We tighten our grips on the chains that hold us here, and we pray – without really believing – for things to improve as we settle for the back and forth.

We have forgotten the truth of momentum, the reality of the pendulum. Instead of seeing life as the ebb and flow, we begin to see it as a treacherous climb followed by an avalanche, and we wonder where we'll ever find the strength to climb again.

Others, more tried and true, teach us to harness our momentum. We can move forward, they say, and certainly higher if only we pump our legs. Bend our knees and throw the force of our bodies into each movement in rhythm with the ride. That, we learn, is the way to change things. That is the way to create more power, to move ourselves, to capture our momentum, and to enjoy the freedom of ever higher flight.

It Is the way to escape.

Swinging high enough, working hard with our own two legs, may eventually give us the strength and the movement to flip right over the bar and come full circle, always moving forward and never back.

At least, that is what the kids on my playground always worked for and always insisted that they had done (when no one was watching). Swinging forward until your feet go over your head and the chains circle the bar was a badge of honor.

It is one we still work for today, as adults, as we listen to the voice of the enemy.

The enemy's voice says our hard work can save us, that it can take away the backward movement and the ebb of life. Pump our legs hard enough, push ourselves high enough, and we will never fall backward again. We can continue moving forward forever as long as we keep our momentum by working our legs with the motion.

We scoff at this as "works-based grace." Then why are we so committed to it?

We aren't, really. Not once it becomes a potential reality. If you have ever watched an older child playing on the swings, he may sometimes boast that he's almost done it: he's about to go full circle and is everyone watching? Just as he goes high enough to swing even with the bar, something in him panics and he tightens his grip and loosens his posture so that the chains slacken and start to dangle, taking away the momentum and the force that could, in theory, grant him his wish.

We don't want to really be upside-down thirty feet in the air. We anticipate the fear we might have when the world goes topsy-turvy and decide to turn back before it's too late. We turn and fight against the energy we labored to build, stop churning our legs, and will our bodies to slow down so that no matter what, we never make it over that bar.

Upside-down, we risk falling. Holding on tight, we know we are safe. Secure, really, and almost comforted by the same tides of life we sought to escape. Thus, we conclude that life is better this way, better with the contrast of good and bad, positive and negative, forward and backward.

But there is another chance of escape, one that thrills us as children but seems senseless as adults. Too much whimsy, we say. Or too dangerous. That's not what swings are for; it is not how it works.

We can just...let go. At the height of our forward motion, in that split second when we hang suspended motionless in the air, we can let go and jump off.

That is what God calls us to do. It is not that He dislikes the ebb and flow of life. Indeed, He created it and set reminders all over the world as the passage from Ecclesiastes reminds us. The sun rises and sets; the tide comes in and out; water flows from river to sea and back again. This is part of God's plan.

His plan is also, though, that we not hold tightly to this life. His plan is not that we not demand our own strength swing us further in either direction. His plan is not that we allow gravity and momentum to hold us down or pull us back.

He created us to fly, to defy gravity itself. He calls us to soar.

There is no greater takeoff than that from momentum, from the height of the greatest swing forward of the pendulum. There, in that split second where physics suspends us, motionless, at the peak, just before gravity starts to pull back down on us, God calls us to let go.

When we let go at that highest height, we do not fall to the ground with a sickening thud. We are propelled forward and the wind catches our hair. We almost soar for just a moment before we focus our attention on this new motion, this forward movement that thrills and terrifies us.

If our feet hit the ground just right, we will instinctively take a couple of steps forward. This is not gymnastics; God does not expect us to stick the landing. No, He wants us to hit the ground running and let the force of our energy keep us moving, pushing forward without much effort at all.

This is how He leads us. It is how He calls us to escape the backs-and-forths and boldly follow Him. It is how we set our example and show that our goal should never be to swing full-circle in ever-moving motion. That will only turn our lives upside-down.

Our call is to let go and burst forth with energy, force, and momentum. Inertia, even, we might say – that our heart in motion will stay in motion.

Our example is a powerful one, prompting those around us to follow suit. Others trapped in the ebb and flow of life's swing now strive to beat our mark, to swing higher before flying off and to land further on the run. To take more steps forward and draw a line in the sand, daring those who follow to beat it.

It becomes a competition, one without the cutthroat misery of struggle and success but a competition of friendly encouragement. We find ourselves standing around in the sand pit, cheering each other on.

Now! we cry. Right now! Let go and jump off! You can make it!

People everywhere are pumping their legs, building their momentum, swinging on life's pendulum, and now waiting for that moment of highest exhilaration when there might not be a better time. There might never be a better opportunity. And then, they let go and soar on the wings of eagles, bask in the breeze, and hit the ground running.

Before we know it, it is our turn again. We fall back into the swing and hold on for dear life, churning our own legs and straining to free ourselves from the vicious cycle. We start to think about circling the bar, about turning everything upside-down in pursuit of perpetual forward motion.

At the last moment, we catch our breath and remember our first time. We remember that feeling of weightlessness, coasting on the air, hearing the cheers of onlookers and the encouragement of witnesses. The time has come, and we must make a choice.

Quickly.

Either we hold tight and let our striving turn everything upside-down. Or we hold tighter but fight against ourselves in a last-ditch attempt to slow down.

Or we simply let go and let ourselves experience that freedom – away from the ebb and flow, away from the back and forth, away from the constant gravity that pulls us back from God's call to fly. And we hit the ground running.

"... They will fly high on wings like eagles. They will run and not grow weary." -Isaiah 40:31b-c

"This is the case of a man who is all alone...yet who works hard to gain as much wealth as he can.... It is all so meaningless and depressing." - Ecclesiastes 4:8

How often have we felt like men (and women) all alone, working hard for something we find in the end to be meaningless? It happens all too often, and part of the problem is the message of the playground.

The world tries to convince us that we are alone, that we can only depend on ourselves to achieve our wildest dreams or to succeed or to find fulfillment. We are all we have ever had and all we ever will have. We are everything, and we are all. We are on one side of the game of life while everyone else runs merrily on the other team.

With a stinging slap across our backs, the world declares, "You're it!."

And we know we must surely be it because it seems the rest of the world starts running away, afraid we might draw them into our game with a simple touch. We are the bottom of the bottom, the least of the least. We watch everyone running in the opposite direction, screaming and laughing like this is so much fun, and the loneliness only sinks deeper into our hearts.

Our eyes search frantically for a target, anything within reach. Anything running around that we might be able to catch up to, and at first, nothing catches our sight. There is that one kid, but he isn't running at all. He probably is not playing.

There are no set rules here; anyone on the field is fair game, but to tag this kid may be in vain. He could just stare back at us, dumbfounded, and declare that he is not playing. Then, we would look foolish, have wasted our energies on yet another meaningless pursuit, and would still be it.

Going after the one kid that isn't running is not wise.

But who are we fast enough to catch, and what are the implications of tagging this player over that one?

Ridding ourselves of being it, freeing ourselves again to run amid the masses and giggle and scream, demands more than a frantic reaching out for anything or anyone that will reach back; it is a move of social strategy. We have to set our sights on someone powerful, a real threat in the open field, and someone well-respected. We have to take on the biggest challenge.

That shows that we can play with the big kids. It shows we have high aspirations, and that we are not afraid of a challenge. It shows passion and commitment to the game, and dedication to playing well.

And won't everyone be impressed when we finally catch up! Tagging that player almost ensures we will be first-picked for every team at every recess to come. It will instill fear in others, and they will want us to be on their side instead of playing against them. We will establish our own reputation as a superstar.

Now, we just have to figure out how to catch up so that we can unburden ourselves from being abandoned and stop being it, stop being all there is and instead run gleefully around while someone else bears the brunt of loneliness and desertion. The idea makes us feel a little guilty, but we understand that the only way to stop being it is to make someone else suffer for awhile, to make someone else run relentlessly and chase and pursue and maybe, yes maybe, even pursue us.

After all, once we catch up, we will be the new superstar, and everyone will want to chase us down.

There is something that satisfies us in watching the mighty fall, until of course, we are the mighty ourselves.

Our jealousy burns as we watch the other players in freedom, still giggling. Still enjoying every minute of it. Always looking around to make sure we're not sneaking up on them, always staying one step ahead so that they are not afflicted by our touch.

It's easy, they shout as they see us begin to grow weary. All you have to do is tag somebody, pass it on, and stop being an outcast. It's entirely in your hands. Just run a little faster and catch up!

Easier said than done as our lungs burn against the air. The other players grow more confident by the minute and are starting to run circles around us, taunting us and reminding us that if we don't step up our game, we will always be it.

You'll never catch me! You'll never catch me! they tease, running close enough to cool us with their breeze but still just out of reach. This seems even more of an excitement to them than the initial game, and they are more drawn to this torture than to the open field.

A question flickers in our heart, wondering why we agreed to play in the first place. We so quickly agreed to being it, to playing this game of chase-the-world and catch up; who convinced us this was best? We could stop at any point, look around at the taunters whose energies are only rising, and with a stone face assert that we are no longer it, that we have decided not to play.

Everyone, in a desperate attempt to save the game and protect their position, would burst out in a chorus of "not it!" until some other poor fool stood alone in the middle of the field with everyone scurrying in the opposite direction.

But to walk away would be to forfeit. We would not solve our problem of feeling alone because we would no longer be just a touch away from the run of the field and the mass of people living on the other side of the game. We would be out. And worse, they would probably never ask us to play again. We would spend the rest of our lives sitting out.

Better to continue the pursuit, to chase our dreams and entertain the possibility of being in the masses, than to eliminate all possibility of that ever happening and condemn ourselves to depressing solitude.

We run until we can't run any more, and we know we will never be fast enough to catch up. Not to the superstar, and maybe not to anyone. Our sights are higher than ever as we continue to think of the glory that will be ours if we can just figure out how to touch that most experienced player, to associate ourselves with that greatness.

Maybe this doesn't need to be a game of speed, we think. Maybe instead of thinking we have to get there now, we could implement some sort of surprise attack and take everyone off guard. It doesn't matter how we obtain our status, so long as we get there and bask in the glory.

We bend over and place our hands on our knees, panting for breath while keeping an eye on our target out of the corner of our eye. Players are starting to slow down, not enough to give up entirely but enough to take the edge out of the game. There, we see him – the one we want to tag.

He is not doing much of anything and hardly has a bead of sweat on him. It is comfortable at the top; you hardly suspect that anyone is coming after you, but you stay paranoid enough to keep one eye on the game. He is looking at us, too.

If we circle around the tree and pause just long enough, maybe he will lose sight of us and let down his guard. We can sneak up behind him and lay a hand gently on his shoulder before he even knows he's caught, before he realizes that power never lasts and finds himself a one-man team with the rest of the world running away. Before he realizes that he's now it, and the entirety of the game is in his hands.

This plan is bound to work, so we take a few more seconds to plan our victory celebration. We will rub it in the faces of the other players, especially the fallen superstar, and proclaim loudly for all to hear that we are the champion. We are the fastest, the strongest, the best player out here, and we did it all ourselves! We were it, and we still managed to come out on top, the envy of the playground and the new powerhouse.

He didn't see us duck behind the tree; we can tell he's looking, but not finding, and that has put him on edge. Our footsteps are soft across the grass, and we are just about there. A few others have noticed what is about to happen and are standing, jaw-dropped, in awe of our brevity and in relief – they know they aren't going to be it.

Their reaction clues him in, and he spins just in time to see us standing there. Before we reach out a finger, he is gone, laughing and giggling and pretending he knew the whole time, that we were never even close.

A large sigh escapes as we feel our fatigue. Being a one-man offense is difficult, and we were so close! We could almost taste our freedom and the relaxing joy of being one of the multitude who simply has to defend themselves. We were almost free of this chasing, almost to a position of being pursued, chased, envied. We were almost in the place where we could be satisfied with what we had and simply make sure we kept it, that we didn't have to be alone again chasing after anything.

Defeat sinks into our spirit, and our steps get heavier. There is not one ounce of run left in us, not one inkling of desire to continue the chase. We are too slow to ever catch up; too slow to tag the superstar, too exhausted to pursue anyone else. We know we are still it, and we resign ourselves to always being alone here, the only one fighting on this side of life, the only one struggling instead of enjoying the game. There is no thrill in the pursuit.

Still, we know we cannot quit. We can never give up because we did not choose this game in the first place; it chose us. Even if we tried to walk away, another unexpected slap across the back would declare us it, and we would find ourselves here again on this lonely side of the game. Fighting, chasing, pursuing, reaching out while everyone else runs away.

There must be a way out of this, a way that puts us back on the whimsical side of things and lets us catch our breath. There must be some way to reach out and touch someone, anyone, and free ourselves.

Then, there he is again – that kid who never bothered to run, who never took off across the field. The one we thought was probably not playing.

It's only fair, we convince ourselves. He's been standing in the middle of the field this whole time; he deserves what is coming to him. Besides, until that stinging slap, nobody told us we were fair game. Nobody told us we were about to be it.

Besides, we continue to rationalize, he's probably used to being a loner, an outsider, a one-man team. He wasn't even invited to play, so he knows what it is to be on the outside. Maybe he'll even appreciate our invitation, even if he has to start on the offensive.

With a weak hand, we reach out and touch the guy, convinced we are doing the right thing.

You're it, we tell him and hope he plays along.
"Fine," He replies. "But no tag backs."

"The one who existed from the beginning is the one we have heard and seen. We saw him with our own eyes and touched him with our own hands." - 1 John 1:1

22 | Teeter-Totter

"Even now my witness is in heaven. My advocate is there on high." - Job 16:19

When the weight of the world weighs us down, where is God? We look up, and it seems He is so far away. The sun shines somewhere behind Him; we can barely make out His form.

Still, we take great comfort in knowing that He is up there, somewhere, beyond and away from this earth. It reminds us that there are many questions we may never answer, problems we may never solve, disasters we may never avert, but our hope is that from His bird's-eye view, He is already taking care of all that.

That is the basis of our faith. It is part of the reason we love God so dearly – we trust Him to exist beyond all measure, beyond all reason, beyond our wildest imaginations. Where our power is lacking, His is strong; where our wisdom fails us, His steadies us.

Yes, we conclude, how blessed are we to have a God so wonderful and even so high. Our Advocate in Heaven.

Our enemy marvels at our conclusion, at how content we are to accept an other-worldly God. He laughs that he's convinced us that Heaven is the best place for the Lord, how we've determined that there is no better place for Him than right where He is: distant and far-removed.

This distant God cannot possibly care about our piddly troubles; He cannot be bothered with our hearts. He is much too busy tending the world to focus on this little speck over that one or one of the many facing tribulation. He is in control, omnipotent, omnipresent, and even omniscient, but all the way up there, He is also impersonal. Yet we fully accept Him as a distant, impersonal advocate.

As long as that is our reaction, as long as we are content in our troubles to throw our hopes into the air, the enemy will continue piling on our burden. More worries. More frustrations. More hate and fear and foolishness. All designed to weigh us down and lift God higher and higher, further and further away from our day-to-day.

Further away from our hearts.

We are content to leave Him there, casting our hopes on the wind and praying they reach Him in time, so long as we continue to make out His form somehow. If we can see that He is still God, that He is still up there, we willingly relegate ourselves to down here.

We understand that we will never fully understand Him, and we appreciate His mystery. Who wants a God that any human can fathom, we question? What kind of God would that even be?

No, it is best this way. It is best He stay where He does the most good – up there, away from here, and where His vision espies the whole world at once.

This kind of hope gives us strength. It gives us the gumption to drag ourselves out of bed every morning, to harness some invisible power that allows us (for a time) to stand up. But because this strength is only the strength of hope and a little faith, it does not draw its power from a true understanding of God. Thus, it is not holy strength.

And it will fail us.

The strength of hope or even of faith, when rooted in a misidentified or distorted God, is nothing more than whatever strength we have in self. We muster it from deep within ourselves and begin, slowly, to believe in it. Not in God, where we assumed we drew our strength from, but in the strength itself.

We believe this strength is enough to sustain us even as we continue longing for the Heavens, for that glorious day of reward when we will finally be as high as God and able to see the world from His view.

Until we get "up there," we think, there is nothing we can understand "down here" that can comfort our heart. God will tell us one day what it all means; He will reveal His methods when we meet Him. For now, we are thankful for our strength and for our assured hope that there is a Heaven.

All of this takes place under our radar, as the world piles on its burdens and holds us more firmly to the ground. It is a heavy way to live. We are tired and troubled.

The more tired and troubled we are, the more we appreciate the Heavens and the idea of our "some day" God.

As we sink into the mire, our own strength fails us, and Heaven can never be close enough. His form fades. We no longer know for sure He is there. This is the trick of our enemy.

He weighs us down until God in the heavens disappears into the sun and we turn our backs in search of something tangible. Our enemy, and his work in this world, are tangible. This is how he steals our hearts.

Thankfully, our God is a God of gravity. He understands the old saying that what goes up must come down. And He's spent all of human history not tucked away in the distant Heavens but walking step-in-step with His people. Not up there, but down here.

That is the beauty of our God.

We cry out to Him, begging Him to come down and answer us. We pray even when His form is nothing but the memory of our vision now imprinted inside of our eyelids. We close our eyes, and the remnants of light outline His majesty in the dark. We continue to cry out until we see Him descend.

He is coming. Truly, He is coming.

The closer He comes, the more we already feel our burdens releasing. With the sight of God in our eyes, the world seems lighter. Almost bearable. Our strength, which was not enough, is taken in by beauty and glory and only made stronger.

Come, Lord! we continue to cry. Come, and never leave me. Bring Your fullness here. Hold my hand and let me hold Yours. Lift this burden. Lord.

He continues to descend, the light of the sun now surrounding Him in brilliance, a magnificent glow. His form grows clearer until He appears before us.

Our burden is lifted, our lives much lighter. Things come into perfect balance as we come face-to-face with the God we were once content to leave in the Heavens, the One that for awhile, we were comfortable not touching but simply holding as a benevolent, though unreachable, Lord.

Suddenly, our feet find their footing. Our legs begin to extend under our weight, finally supporting us. Finally giving us room to move out of the mire. Finally, with the way God is sharing our burden, we embrace true strength.

We watch in awe and wonder how He is doing that. How is He sharing our burden, lifting the weight off our shoulders, while He's still over there? No longer up there; down here, but still a few feet away.

Then, we see. His feet, too, are firmly planted on the ground. His feet, too, stand in the mire. It is the union of our strength with His that gives us the balance to stand. It is our shared commitment, our covenant, that steadies our hearts, our minds, and our understanding.

Without God's willingness to come down and set His feet in the muck, we would be sinking ever deeper under our burden until the mud covered our eyes and we could not see Him at all.

Our burden is no different. Though we now stand, it is not because He has removed it from us. No, He has come instead with the weight of His holiness – His tender mercies, His perfect strength, His magnificent plan – and brought nothing more than balance and new perspective.

Perspective that brings Him down from way up there in contrast to our troubles to now look us gently in the eye and reassure us. His goodness perfectly answers our burden on the fulcrum of faith.

For a bit, we rest there. We thank Him for His awesomeness, His willingness to come down from Heaven and stabilize our lives. As we look across the small space that separates us, we see in His eyes the realness of His power. His wisdom, mercy, gentleness, and righteousness stare back at us in a way that takes our breath away. It humbles us.

Instead of falling to our knees and praising Him, we find that we are almost floating. Burdens and all. He paints a stark contrast against the mire that sinks behind Him, the beauty so awe-inspiring that we have no words as our feet leave the ground.

Where are we going? we wonder. Why is it that God is now sinking where it should have been us?

He is not sinking, we realize when our eyes focus on the ground expanding before us. His feet have not moved but remain where they were: solidly on the ground. His legs bend with the weight of His being.

Our feet dangle carelessly over the edge and now our burden is so light we can hardly feel it. The wind whips through our hair in a cool and refreshing breeze.

He knows to sink gently, knows that His increasing presence raises us higher. Too quickly or too hard, and He'll do nothing but catapult us across creation.

We soar, but only as He allows as we come to understand the true weight of His wholeness. His beauty. His grace. His redemption. His power. His strength. When these become real to us, real in a way that we can no longer deny or ignore, then the heavy reality of a loving God causes a dramatic shift in the balance of our faith.

We regret the time we spent in the mire, letting life's troubles weigh us down. We understand how watching God ascend higher into the Heavens with each disappointment was nothing short of underestimating His power. The only reason we fell was because we failed to believe God could be bigger than our problems or our worries.

They were never too big for Him; we simply had to invite Him, through prayer, to provide the balance. When He does, we come to see that He is bigger and greater and yes, even heavier, than all things. His size and power and might outweigh our doubts and fears so that when we put Him in His rightful place, His trueness lifts us up.

Higher, higher, higher we soar, knowing that as long as God rests down here, as long as He acts as the balancing power in our lives, we will never fall. We will never sink under anything the enemy throws at us or under life's stresses. We will never again float our hopes aimlessly into the sky, praying for an advocate somewhere "up there."

We will know that our Advocate is here, right here on the playground with us. He is holding down His end of the covenant so that, by faith, we can fly. Where the air is clear, the breeze is cool, and the scenery breathtaking. Where no care weighs us down because no care outweighs our God.

If ever we forget or begin to question His role in the matter, we must only look across our faith to see Him sitting on the other side, just who He says He is and who we believe He is and who He has always promised to be: the balance in our lives.

"You have allowed me to suffer much hardship, but you will restore me to life again and lift me up from the depths of the earth." - Psalm 71:20

23 | Tetherball

"How foolish to trust in something made by your own hands! What fools you are to believe such lies!"

– Habakkuk 2:18b

We know that our complete fulfillment rests somewhere in the Heavens, where there is a God watching out for our best interests and orchestrating the universe to bless His children.

Yet we cannot help but yearn for some of that goodness to reach down here. We don't want it to lose its supernatural foundation, but we would like to know what is going on. We want something tangible, something besides hope and the vague idea that He might be up to something.

So He drops us a ball, a blessed gift of the Holy Spirit that could lead us down the right path or answer a long-burning question in our heart, but which is still firmly tethered high beyond our reach. Knowing that this perfect gift (for what other shape would be perfect but the exact roundness of a ball) cannot crash against the ground and shatter is comforting.

This is not something lifted up; it is an answer come down.

Our hearts leap and we jump instinctively toward it, thankful for something so wonderful and for the God who hears and answers our prayers. We hold that ball in our hands for a few moments, turning it this way and that while admiring its perfectness. Our eyes follow the string that holds it in place until the sun becomes so blinding that we must turn away.

We know that where we are blinded by the powerful light, the goodness of God is only beginning; we can hardly contain our excitement.

The more we ponder this beautiful thing we hold in our hands, that we are not even permitted to walk away with but that we can only stand and admire, the more we wonder if it is too good to be true. It is everything we asked for, everything we imagined. Could we be fooling ourselves into believing it?

We look into our hands and see something too good, too perfect. It is our dream come true, dangling in front of us in suspended animation, and it is tied here. It is stuck firmly in this ground, we begin to understand as we shift our eyes from the end of the tether to the base of the pole. And all of a sudden, we start to feel a little foolish.

This is a product of our own making. That's why it seems to be so perfect and answers so much of the depths of our spirit – we created it just as we wanted it to be. We took our prayers and our hopes and our imaginations and brought them to life, planted and even cemented into the very ground we walk on and created the illusion that it comes from above with a simple tether. One flimsy little rope that disappears into the sun's reflection on the metal of the pole and could probably snap without much effort.

Oh, our foolishness! To believe that God would ever answer us so wonderfully! This is no gift from our

Father; it is a trap of the Devil. And we curse God for having let this all happen.

We drop the ball and let it just dangle there in front of us, not touching the ground but no longer captivating our interest. Except that out of our hands, it never stops dancing like a gnat buzzing around our eyes.

There is no walking away. Not now.

Maybe it is not holy or righteous. Maybe it was never an answer from God but was only a figment of our own deep yearning. But at the very least, it has given us a stronger idea of our own desires and of the way we long for God to respond. This is now a good idea we can bat around with the Lord while we figure out what else to do with it.

Why can't you answer me like this, Father? we ask. And why is the pain in my heart only deepening the longer I stand here looking at this ball? Free me from my rush to fulfillment and my foolishness! I only want what is of You!

We play with the ball a little as it continues to hang there, bouncing in the gentle wind. We hold it in our hands awhile longer, looking again at its perfectness and aching because we know we are only fooling ourselves. If we consider it, we remember when this land was barren, when there was no pole here at all. And we remember watching the man pour the cement to put this in the ground.

How could we have ever thought this could be from God? The pole came first; the tether second; the ball last. This was built from the ground up.

The ball shifts between our hands, first to the left and then to the right as we ponder it endlessly, simultaneously wishing it was from God and the answer we were seeking while not allowing ourselves the delusion.

Around the pole it goes, wrapping and unwrapping as we toss it between our hands. On the one hand, we say as it lands in our right palm, God could simply be waiting on my initiative. If I take the first step and hold this as my own, perhaps He will bless it anyway and do something beyond my wildest imagination.

On the other hand, we counter ourselves as the ball nestles atop our left fingers, it could be nothing more than a test or my projection of my own will on a God I am making in my image. If I hold this as my own, it may bring a curse to bear.

It is a tough dilemma, one we debate for hours standing in the hot sun, batting the ball back and forth without letting it get tangled around itself or its grounding.

But we cannot stand here forever. We could try, but we would never get anywhere as long as we remain unwilling to let our dream travel any further than one hand to the other; as long as we continue contradicting our own every thought, we will never score a single point.

And what is to say that in all of our fiddling, we will not break the string and let our dream crash to the ground as we have always feared? The more we play with it without knowing its game, the likelier we are to send it shattering.

As that thought strikes us, we look again at this so-called good and perfect gift. It's starting to go flat here on this one side, and there's a little scuff mark over here. Someone must have pounded it too hard or caught it on the ring of their hand because there's a long gouge on this side. And the air inlet is starting to bulge out, probably from years of reinflation.

This is no good and perfect gift; it might still be slightly good, but it is no longer perfect. The longer we look at it, the more its flaws begin to show.

Disappointed, we let it fall to the end of its tether and again dangle in the breeze. It still bounces, dancing and taunting us, but we know we have wasted our time here – here with this manmade pole that grounded our dream though we tried to make it appear from above; here with this imperfect imposter posing as something wonderful.

In a fit of fury, we curse the ball and all it ever represented. With a good hard final whack, we condemn it to be bound in this place forever, grounded and tangled and never to dance or entice us again, and part of us wishes the string would break as it whips around and around and around and send that ball flying into outer space.

We turn to walk away, and the accursed thing whops us right in the back of the head.

Perfect, we mumble to ourselves while we rub the stinging wound. Just perfect.

"Yes, it is," God answers.

It is? It is what?

"It is perfect."

But this was just my own whimsy, we reply. This was my fantasy come to life and projected onto you. I watched the man cement this pole into the ground and secure the tether to the top. How could this have been Your perfect gift?

"Did you see the man's face?"

We admit that we had not; he had been too engrossed in the work, and we had paid little mind to him except to notice he was up to something.

He goes on to explain that He was that man, that this has been His plan from the very beginning, from Creation itself. He knew that He had to come down here and establish His presence firmly in this world, but He also knew that after man had fallen, He could not stay. His power was needed in the Heavens to work on our behalf.

But He always heard us. That is why He sent this gift. This good and perfect gift that He tethered to His presence in this world by the gift of His Spirit, our lifeline to the Heavens.

This perfect, beautiful gift that we turned over and over in our hands and our hearts until it was no longer perfect and no longer a gift.

We look back at the ball, still wrapped tightly around the pole and dangling but no longer dancing. There is not enough slack left to make it dance.

Maybe we have actually done well, we tell ourselves as our new understanding takes hold. We wanted to tie up this gift, to make sure it could never toy with our hearts again nor anyone else's. Now, we have wrapped it around the establishment of God and kept it close to its source so that even though it is not free to dance, it is somehow more secure by the mixing of His Spirit and His presence. We got the point.

God only laughs.

A little boy runs by and swats the ball in the other direction, letting it gently unwind from its frozen state, and it is free to bounce and jiggle and dance again, enticing us to return.

God invites us to come to the holy place where His presence is grounded and His Spirit secures our hopes, our dreams, and our wildest imaginations, and He tells us to take hold of this gift.

As we do, we look again at what we had always hoped was our gift but could not dare to believe. It is not imperfect, we realize, though it is still scuffed and scratched and going flat over here and bulging over there. It is well-worn, a gift that has been shared with millions of God's children for thousands of years. He has now seen fit to deliver it here to this place, in this time, specifically for us.

We bat it again, inviting it to dance. This time, we look to put our own mark on it. That maybe someday when another of God's children finds this good and perfect gift, they will see another mark of His perfectness in its imperfections.

"Whatever is good and perfect comes to us from God above, who created all heaven's lights."- James 1:17

24 | Wacky Races

"Don't you realize that in a race everyone runs, but only one person gets the prize? So run to win!"

– 1 Corinthians 9:24

Run to win. Isn't that how it always is?

Gone are the days of running for the sake of, well, running. Of feeling the wind through our hair and chapping our cheeks; of feeling the power of our legs churning beneath us. There is no joy left in running.

We run to win.

Nobody runs laps at recess. Where is the challenge, the thrill of the competition? Where is the victory? We grab a friend or two, huddle together on the far corner of the playground, and dare them: "Bet I can get to that tree before you! Ready, go!"

Our "go" comes before they've accepted the challenge, before they've figured out which tree we were pointing at. Before they've tied their shoes tight or caught their breath.

Nobody said the race had to be fair. Nobody said there were rules. It's about one thing and one thing only: getting to that little tree before anybody else. That makes us the ruler of the playground. That makes us the king of recess. That solidifies our status.

We're not just the fastest. We're the fastester. We invented the word to make sure everyone understands our superiority; there is no room for doubt. We are it.

We are fastester.

And that is how we run our race. Time slips into eternity while we pound our feet on the ground and push forward, always looking back over one shoulder to make sure no one is catching up. That we're not in danger of losing our lead.

We neglect the miracle of our bodies. We reject the limits of our strength and endurance. We push ourselves beyond all reasonable limits for the chance to win. Winning is the payoff; it is the return on our investment.

Our too many hours at the office should pay off with a promotion or a pay raise. Our nights lying awake next to our spouse should pay off in fidelity and a long marriage. Our over-extended volunteerism at church should nominate us for sainthood. Or maybe not right away, but after something tragic happens and those heathens realize they'd never have made it without us.

Sadly, we rarely see the finish line. The race ends, for us, when we fall face-first into the pavement. We finally find rest in death, confident and content in our performance and somehow satisfied that we, alone, led the pack. That we were in first with no one in our rear-view mirror, no one threatening to overtake us.

Our fatal flaw is our assumption that the rest of the world runs our course, that they must be behind us, following, struggling to catch up because there is only one race. Only one finish line.

This is when God steps in and turns what we believed to be a straight-up sprint into a wacky race.

My dad swore he invented the wacky race, but I'm

sure it's a common concept. Whenever we'd have a few minutes, standing around not doing much of anything, waiting on this or that thing to happen so we could rush into our next project, our next meeting, our next deadline, dad set up a wacky race.

The rules were simple: dad stood in the middle as the start and finish line and the referee. He'd point out two destinations, one to his left and one to his right. Putting a kid at each of his heels, he shouted a start signal. I took off to the left; another poor sap to the right. When we reached the pre-set end point, we turned around and sped past dad and past each other to the other side. Whoever hit both points and returned to dad first was the winner.

There was no good way of knowing, at any given time, who was ahead. Who was winning.

That made wacky races very frustrating and almost no fun.

Don't get me wrong – we still ran to win. We always ran to win. It was just that something changed without the hot breath of a worthy opponent breathing down your neck, their hard footsteps echoing in your ears, and that shot of panic when you turn back for a split second to realize they are, quite literally, right on your heels.

When the race turns wacky, you've got to throw all that aside and race for yourself. You run your own course. You run it hard because you run to win, but you know you're the only one out there.

Determination sets in. The instinct to run with every ounce of strength and speed in our being takes over and propels us toward the finish line with beads of sweat pouring down our faces, stinging in our eyes. Our chests burn with the breathlessness of our striving. Dizziness rushes in and blurs our vision, but only for a moment, until we shake it off and refocus our energies on the end. The finish line.

The Father standing in the middle, both the beginning and the end.

Suddenly, that's all we're running for – for the outstretched arms that point the way to the distances, the arms that stand ready to receive us.

We're running even harder now, yearning for the finish line as it comes into sight. It's not clouded by expectation; there are no remaining thoughts of that promotion at work, that perfect family, that anointing into sainthood, or the millions of other selfish things we used to run for. Our striving is for righteousness, for finishing for finishing's sake, and we are free once again to concentrate on the power in our legs.

An instinctual glance toward the competition, an opponent whose race ran a different course, does not dissuade our hearts, though we watch them cross the finish line first. It's not in us to give up. Not now.

Not while He's standing there, patiently awaiting our arrival. Not while our opponent stands cheering us on, encouraging us to run harder, faster. There's something new in the camaraderie of the race, in the way the competition has all but faded.

We still want to win; we want that prize. But our prize is different now, better than any ribbon or trophy or the satisfaction of coming in first.

Our prize is the welcome of those outstretched arms that embrace our tired, sweaty bodies in perfect rest. A heart willing to press against our own in an incredible syncopated rhythm. Living water that rehydrates our spirits. A touch that brings our second wind and plasters a small, wry smile across our faces.

It is a smile that says, without a second thought to tired legs, "I could do that again. Right now. I could run this wacky race to my Father forever and never grow weary."

That is the only race He's ever called us to run.

Too many of us are guilty of spending our lives racing to win, to get ahead, to stay one step in front of the competition. We run the race looking backward, keeping an eye on any threats to our supremacy. The people who mean the most to us are often the ones who most feed our egos, and we are dying to leave a legacy of something grand. Literally dying chasing a legacy of the best ever, the greatest, the wealthiest, the busiest.

The fastester.

But how many of us would be truly satisfied or even proud of ourselves if we finished that race, collapsed well before the finish line, and met God only to have Him look us in the eye, shake His head, and say, "Well, you did it. You were the fastester."

Imagine how disappointed, how let down you would be if that's all He could say about your life.

We want to believe there is something more to us, something beyond what we can achieve. Beyond the hours we can put in at the office. Beyond the pursuit of our one perfect mate. Beyond children who are doctors and lawyers.

Somewhere deep within us, we know this is the truth. We know we are more than the straight-up race would tell us. We know we've got much more to offer than a paycheck or an annual report. But to pursue anything less would be countercultural at best, devastating at worst.

Devastating because as aware as we are that there's something more to us than credentials, we are equally aware that we'll never come close to maximizing our potential. We will never be as disciplined, devout, or successful as we want to be. Our faith will sometimes fail us. Our hearts will grow weary; we will near fainting. We'll reach that point where we want to just throw our hands in the air and give up because pursuing fastester is too painstaking.

We strive for holiness, but the world's race is never holy. Holy comes when the race turns wacky. Holy comes when our sweat mixes with His blood. Holy is the fire that won't let us quit. Holy is the passion that drives us to run our hardest, hearts reaching out for righteousness, for the chance to touch our Father.

I'm sure that Paul, who wrote most frequently about the Christian journey as a race, would have counted among his joys not just his imprisonment, persecution, and poverty, but also the heaving, heavy chest of breathlessness, the pounding heart of exertion, and the ache of exhausted muscles.

Paul knew. He understood how crucial the race was. He understood the drive in each of us to cross the finish line. He understood that his audiences – in Philippi, Galatia, Ephesus, across the Christian world – could appreciate the analogy. They would understand, he absolutely knew, the training that goes into the race, the anticipation of the challenge, the dedication of the runner, even the call to be the fastester.

God knows, too. He understands what drives us, and that is why He uses our own inclinations to His advantage. He uses our own desires to draw us deeper into relationship with Him.

He knows we can't just take off out of the gates and run the fastest race, even though we want to. That's why He lets us practice, pointing a short distance one direction and a bit further the other way. We come back to Him in between, encouragement along the way, always pushing ourselves a little further by His hand. He expects us to go just where He's sent us, then fly back by en route to where else He sends us. And maybe He'll send us back the other direction, further still, until this routine settles into us.

Go where God's sent me. Remember to come back to Him. Go where He's sent me. Remember to come back to Him.

He also knows how we compare ourselves to others, how we watch them and yearn for this or that in their lives. That is why He never sends any two of us in the same direction. Not at the same time. He knows to take the competition out of it so that we learn to seek righteousness, to run toward God with the fullness of our being for no other reason than to satisfy that tender yearning of our hearts.

He knows to use the strength and self-discipline and determination and seeming tirelessness that defines the world's race, the one we get caught up in right at the starter's pistol when the doctor slaps our hind ends, to cultivate faith.

He knows we're going to run anyway, either to Him or away from Him, stumbling ahead of the pack or steadily eyeing the finish line.

He knows we have to run a wacky race.

"I strain to reach the end of the race and receive the prize for which God, through Christ Jesus, is calling us up to heaven."– Philippians 3:14

Epilogue | When the Whistle Blows...

When the whistle blows, the time for games ends and we are left standing out of breath. Our hearts pound hard as we walk toward the refuge of the building, away from the harsh elements of the playground.

It is an easy place to lose yourself, we conclude with a look over our shoulder. The time went by too fast. And all we have to show for our frivolity is a heaving chest that almost burns with the sting of fresh air and a pounding heart fresh off the exhilaration of conquest, triumph and defeat, and aimless fun.

Now, here we stand with one hand on the door and a longing still in our eyes. We know what we could have done better out there, and we have a pretty good idea how things might have gone worse. We know that if we had just five more minutes, we would do some things differently.

We would pursue our dreams with more passion, perhaps. We would have been nicer to the kid picked last for every team. We would have shown more humility in victory and discipline in defeat. We would not neglect to take a minute and look around, to notice those things around us that we missed the first time because we were too driven and too focused on our own goals. On playing our own games.

We would have seen the way the clouds parted with a thin band of gold encasing the shadows on each side.

We would have watched the birds flitter from tree to tree, the squirrels shimmering up the tree trunks with acorns in their mouths. We would have paid attention to the interplay of weeds and grass under our feet and caught a glimpse of the wind demolishing a dandelion.

Yes, we would do a thing or two differently if we had more time. If we had just one more chance. But our time is up. The whistle has blown, that shrill sound that stopped everything in its tracks and sent us scrambling for the door.

It is hard to go in. Something inside us, something frantic but unspoken, wants to hold onto this. This...emptiness, we suddenly realize. That is what is holding us here; not the memory of our pleasure but the emptiness that taunts us.

Unfinished business, we decide. We remember so clearly that every moment our muscles churned, every step ahead that we plotted in our minds, every team we picked by schoolyard rules, every strategic, tactical, or seemingly irrelevant move we made out here had a purpose. At the time, we knew what we were working toward and how each little step would propel us to that goal.

Now, we cannot remember what it was that drew us into the game. We don't remember why we started playing or what our goal was, though we realize almost instantly that we never reached it. There is something hollow about standing here, waiting to leave the playground, and knowing that all that seemed so purposeful and edifying is clearly meaningless.

We played the games. We played by the rules that just about everyone agreed to, rules that were set generations before we ever arrived in this place. Not only did we play by the rules; we gave it our all. We played to win.

We played for the honor. We played for the power. We played for success and comfort and pleasure. We played for status.

Yet here we stand, surrounded by those who never played fairly. They broke the rules at every turn and seemed like they were leading when the whistle blew.

There are those here who played without playing, who ran roughshod over the rest of us and somehow made it out on top, though none of us understood how or why.

There are those here who played an entirely different game, amateurs we call them. They could not have broken any rules because they never understood them, but we let them play partially out of pity and partially because we knew they would never be a threat.

There are those here who never played at all. They walked around oblivious to the difficulty of our game and shook their heads in a sad sort of way. They never joined in, never even asked to join, but simply stood watching with no chance to win. They never gunned for anybody, never took a risk, never used a single muscle and therefore never appreciated the difficulty of the game.

And there are those, at least there is One, who... well, nobody really knows what He was doing.

He never played to win, and He never played for keeps. He wandered around, sticking His hand in a game here and there but only long enough to turn the tide. As we wait for the door to open, He has a silly sort of smile on His face and remains separate, apart. He's crouched down in the dirt where millions of footprints cross one another, and He's dabbling with something.

He is not doing as most of us would do and starting with a clean slate, running His hands over the ground to make a smooth canvas. Instead, He leaves it just as it is and begins with one finger to move the little dust around, creating…Heaven knows what.

He is going to get in trouble, we think. He did not come and line up when recess was over. For a minute, we are jealous, knowing that He has done exactly what we wanted to do and stayed out there. He is taking these extra moments, this second chance, this last-ditch effort to do things differently. And we? We stand waiting at the door with one sad eye always looking back.

Then, the door swings open. Just inside lies the place of all knowledge.

Our Teacher greets us near the open door, shooing us inside with a smile and watching our weary little bodies file past one by one by one. He knows we are tired. He knows we outdid ourselves out there, pushed ourselves too hard. He knows that we wish we had five more minutes, that we feel like we fell just short of whatever goal it was we were working toward. He knows, and His eyes dance with sympathy behind that grin.

The smile is welcoming, comforting. We feel known, simply known and not judged. In a split second, it takes away any discomfort we have ever had with our Teacher.

For the longest time, we were intimidated by Him. It was everything about Him – the way He stood while the rest of us were required to sit, the way He moved while we were still, the way He posed questions we felt inadequate to answer. He was always patient, always encouraging and a commanding presence. But we were always a little scared by Him.

Maybe we feared most His red pen and knowing that with a single stroke, He could either pass or fail us.

Now, while we watch His knowing barely masked in His eyes behind that smile, that fear simply vanishes. We are overwhelmed by His gentleness and mercy. Our whole spirit sinks in a visible sigh as we relax in His presence. The red pen stays clipped in His pocket, as it always has, and we almost chuckle at it now.

We remember every word He has written with that pen, every stroke we have seen scrawled out before us that we were afraid to look at but knew would strengthen us.

The silent chuckle spreads a smile across our face, and we look up. Our smile is partly our amusement, our recognition of the feebleness of our wisdom, and partly the contagiousness of His pearly whites.

A second lasts an eternity, our eyes meeting His and accepting a silent invitation to listen, to learn. This is our Teacher, we think, having never known a greater truth. It is not just compassion that dances behind those eyes; it is knowledge.   More specifically, it is wisdom.

We sit eagerly, waiting on Him to speak while faint memories of our exploits on the playground replay in our minds.   Recess was long anticipated, but this moment had not been on our radar. Or if it had, it had been stifled by our questions about the depth of this Teacher's wisdom. We had thought He might teach us, but we were more confident we might teach Him a thing or two.

The irony of the burning in our faces, the way they beat red as the wind and the sun have chapped them, is not lost in this moment, sitting at our Teacher's feet.

While we wait, anxious for Him to speak, the million questions we would ask ourselves if we were in His shoes roll through our minds. Was it worth it? we would ask. That would be enough. We can already feel ourselves swallowing one last hard swallow before breaking into a lengthy justification of our every action, every move we made in a fruitless game that seemed so important at the time.

When finally He speaks, it is His compassion that is loudest. Backed by the eyes that knew us the moment we entered this place, He speaks simple words:

"Welcome, children."

And this place of all knowledge, where we feared a pop quiz none of us felt adequately studied for, reveals the knowledge itself and answers our questions, even the ones we were afraid to ask.

It answers our questions about our strife, about the fruit of our labors or lack thereof, about those who break the rules and come out on top and those living lives of discipline who never catch a break. It answers our questions about our place and most importantly, our worth. It answers our questions about victory and defeat, gains and losses, and the meaning behind everything we think we have worked toward. It answers the questions of our heart, sometimes without a single word, and resolves every questioning conflict.

We hear our Teacher's story, for the first time, addressing the thousands of questions we have wanted to ask about the days He wandered this same playground.

Our hearts soak in that knowledge in peace and in grace, and we know we would sit at this Teacher's feet forever.

Then, we remember another Man. He was the one who would not come in, who did not heed the piercing sound of the whistle. He was the one who would not even clear our footprints from the ground before adding His own touches, His own artistic finesse. He was the one, we assume, who was still crouched outside in the dirt. He was the one whose countenance mimicked that of our Teacher – silently strong, persistently purposeful, oddly strange but contagious and yes, enviable.

This truth that is now settling into our hearts is one He would identify with, we think before realizing He doesn't need to hear this truth; He is already living it.

We remember this Man who we thought would get in trouble, who would cause a panic as people searched high and low for Him. We remember thinking He was rebellious, obstinate, and even pitiful because He was not willing to come inside.

We remember thinking that He was soaking in every extra moment, every last-ditch effort, every second and third and fourth chance to hang on.

We remember, and for His patience, His persistence, His steadfast unwillingness to abandon His world, and His doodling in the dirt – for the fullness of His presence - we rejoice.

ABOUT THE AUTHOR

Aidan Rogers is a young author from the heartland of America. She holds a Bachelor's degree in journalism from Franklin College, where a wise professor warned her that if she did not control her wordplay, it would control her. She used that as motivation to harness God's call to the beautiful gift of language.

Since coming to Christ as a teenager, Aidan has written a series of devotionals and has been active in drama ministry and public speaking.

Recess is Aidan's third completed manuscript but the first work she has published. The first two, she says, were the stories she had to get out of the way to make sure the rest of her words were purely God's. She has three other manuscripts in development, including a sequel - *Rainy Day Recess: Indoor Games with God.*

Aidan welcomes feedback and inquiry. Contact her via email at communicaidan@hotmail.com.

11784593R0012

Made in the USA
Lexington, KY
01 November 2011